**Dedicated
to the memory of**

Jane S. Pinheiro

Wildflower Artist

For whom the Interpretive Center at the California State Poppy Reserve was named.

In this book I have quoted extensively from an unpublished manuscript Jane wrote which was meant to be an adjunct to some of her wildflower paintings. All quotations from Jane's manuscript are reproduced as they appear in the original. The title is:

*A Bug's Eye View of Some Desert
Miniatures and a Giant Lily.*

Wildflower Photography

Wildflowers can be some of the most beautiful photographic subjects. At times they may be the most frustrating. Some blue flowers, especially those with shading on the purple side, will photograph pink or red. This is especially true of Blue Dicks, Chinese Houses, Thistle Sage and a number of Lupine. Mesa Phlox is an electric blue, but it tends to photograph a dull gray. An explanation for this is that film is sensitive to colors that the eye does not see. In this book, you will find flowers in the blue section which look red. Please take my word for it: They are blue or at least a bluish-purple.

When photographing wildflowers, my recommendation is to shoot with a macro lens and to use Kodachrome 200 film. The macro lens allows you to photograph the minute details of the flower and the fast film enables you to stop motion caused by the wind (which seems to always blow in the spring), and to get the greatest depth of field. The Kodachrome film probably records the color more realistically than does other film. However, do not expect even that film to record all colors correctly.

Flowerwatcher Publishing Co.
45026 11th St. West
Lancaster, CA 93534

Art Production and Printing Coordination
by Creative Ideals, Inc.
432 F Street Suite 505
San Diego, CA 92101

TABLE OF CONTENTS

PREFACE

To be able to call the plants by name makes
them a hundredfold more sweet and intimate.
Naming things is one of the oldest and simplest
of human pastimes.

Henry Van Dyke, in *Little Rivers*

This book is written for people with no botanical knowledge who happen to be curious about the common name of a wildflower they might find in the Antelope Valley. In an area of such rich botanical resources as is this Valley (at least in years of average or better rainfall), experience has shown that a book which helps identify at least the common wildflowers is very much needed. As a non-botanist wildflower photographer for over 20 years, I have found that no one wildflower book for the lay person—or even four or five—lists all of the more prominent wildflowers in this area.

Although this text emphasizes the common names of flowers, I have also included the botanical names (from A Flora of Southern California by Dr. Philip A. Munz, University of California Press, 1974) should the reader wish to further investigate a particular plant. Because of the difficulty of describing the features of some plants, I have had to use some botanical terms. A glossary of these terms is found on page 9. As many common names as are known are given along with the one used most frequently in the Antelope Valley as the heading. Another reason for including botanical names is that the same common name may be applied to a number of flowers whereas botanical names are very specific.

It is estimated that there are some 2,200 different kinds of wild plants growing in the Antelope Valley and the surrounding foothills. To help the reader identify all of these plants is very much beyond the scope of this book. To simplify identification, I have limited myself to about 193 of the most common and significant spring-blooming wild plants.

The area covered by this book is the Antelope Valley, the surrounding foothills and the canyons leading into the Valley. This area is roughly from Gorman on the west to the Los Angeles County line on the east and from California City on the north to the foothills and canyons on the south.

The Antelope Valley is a unique wildflower growing area mainly because of the varying amounts of rainfall and temperatures. Because of this, certain flowers may be common and plentiful on one side of the Valley and never be seen on the other side of the Valley. The freeway and railroad tracks

4

seem to be the rough dividing line for this phenomenon. One of the means used to identify flowers in this book is to give the general location where they are **most likely** to be found. However I do not claim that the location indicated is the only place they will be found.

Every wildflower year is different in regard to which wildflowers are dominant and which ones are growing. All of this depends not only on the amount of rain or snow, but also when it falls, the temperature during the rainy season and the types of soil. **Every year is a new adventure!** Every wildflower has its own "clock." It will bloom whenever conditions meet the needs of that flower, and conditions will vary a great deal from one flower to another. Seeds of some wildflowers have been known to lie dormant for 30 years or more and then burst forth into glorious bloom. In 1990, a year of little rain, I have been most amazed to find at least six species of wildflowers which we have never seen before in more than 20 years of flowerwatching. Obviously, I have not included them in this book because they are rare. But don't be surprised if you too find a flower which is not in this publication. When you do, I suggest that you photograph it if possible, write down a description of the plant (flowers, height, shape of leaves and so on), with when and where you found it, so that other flower-watchers may help you identify the plant. It is always so satisfying, when you can solve the mystery of "What is the name of that plant?"

We sincerely hope that this publication will help you to solve many of these mysteries.

ACKNOWLEDGEMENTS

Many persons have given me help and encouragement in the preparation of this book. I particularly wish to thank the following people:

Marie Zaferis, my fellow photographer and self-taught botanist, who was my main consultant as to what flowers should be in this book, where they grow and so on and who provided 58 photographs used in this book. She is a good friend and a truly remarkable lady.

Dr. Bob Gustafson, botanist, Los Angeles County Natural History Museum for his help in identifying certain flowers. Quotations in the book identified as his statements are from letters to Marie Zaferis.

Wandalee Thompson, self-taught botanist, who over the years has given me the most help in learning about Antelope Valley wildflowers and who gave valuable advice and information about specific flowers in this book.

Dorothy Bolt, chairperson of the Wildflower Preservation Committee of the Lancaster Woman's Club, who gave me a great deal of support and encouragement in this effort and who helped select the photographs for the book.

Joyce Bowman, who helped select the photographs for the book.

Josephine Williams, for her support and encouragement.

William De Witt, who half-toned the photocopies of the wildflowers and who produced the map on page 160.

John Stark, my botanist-trained son, who made valuable suggestions as to the format of the book and as to the descriptions of the various plant families.

Mary Austin, Jeanne Sherman and **Doreen Settle,** for information contained in questionnaires.

Heidi Preschler, Professor of English at Antelope Valley College, for proofreading the book.

Milt McAuley, for his invaluable instructions about techniques of publishing. Milt has written and published the following books:

Wildflowers of the Santa Monica Mountains
Hiking Trails of the Santa Monica Mountains
Hiking in Topanga State Park
Hiking Trails of Point Mugu State Park
Hiking Trails of Malibu Creek State Park
Wildflower Walks of the Santa Monica Mountains
Guide to the Backbone Trail of the Santa Monica Mountains
Information about these books may be obtained from Canyon Publishing Co., 8561 Eatough Ave., Canoga Park, CA 91304

PHOTOGRAPHIC CREDITS

ABOUT THE AUTHOR

Milt Stark has lived in the Antelope Valley area since 1923. He received his B.A. degree from the University of Southern California and worked most of his adult life as a deputy probation officer and administrator of various probation camps. It was while he was Director of Camp Mendenhall in Lake Hughes, when inspecting work crew projects in the Angeles National Forest and working with the camp nursery, that he became interested in native plants as photographic subjects. This, together with his curiosity as to the names of the plants he was photographing, lead to his botanical investigations.

He was a member of the Wildflower Preservation Committee while they were raising money to help buy the land for the State Poppy Reserve. He was chairman of the Antelope Valley State Parks Advisory Committee and was master of ceremonies at the bicentennial dedication of the California State Poppy Reserve. He has been co-leader of the Wild-flower Bus Tours sponsored by the Theodore Payne Foundation for more than 12 years. For at least 15 years he has narrated a slide show entitled The Folklore of Antelope Valley Wildflowers for a variety of school and community groups, first to publicize the activities of the Wildflower Preservation Committee, and later to publicize the work of the West Antelope Valley Historical Society, of which he is past president. He served on the Board of the Westside Elementary School District for 12 years. He does not claim to be a botanist, but rather a photographer who is fascinated with the history and folklore of our native plants.

HOW TO USE THIS BOOK

I suggest the following steps in using this book to identify a flowering plant:

1. Look through the photographs to find a look-alike flower. The photographs of herbaceous plants are arranged by color with the **yellow to orange** flowers first, followed by **red to purple, blue to lavender,** and then **white to cream**. The last section is of nonherbaceous plants which are **trees, shrubs, vines** and **cacti**. Underneath each photograph is a common name and the page number on which the description of the plant is found. **I strongly suggest that, after identifying a flower from the photograph, you always check the description of the flower.** A number of plants have flowers that look the same, but have leaves or other parts of the plant which are differently shaped. Many of the descriptions also include information about how the Indians used the plant or how it got its name.

2. Within each color section, the plants are arranged by the number of petals. They are in ascending order, with those having no petals at the beginning and those having the most petals at the end.

3. The color photographs give the shape and color of the flower. The text gives a description of the flower after the heading **Fls.,** the height of the plant after **Ht.,** a description of the leaves after **Lvs.** and the areas where the plant is most likely to be found after **Areas**. (Please refer to the Antelope Valley map on page 160 for designated areas.) All of these items are important in flower identification. In addition, next to almost half of the plants described is an illustration (actually a reduced photocopy of the plant), indicating the structure of the plant and the leaf shape.

4. Descriptions of plants are organized by families beginning with those families having no petals or no apparent petals, and ascending to those families with the most petals. In the text portion of the book are descriptions of various plant families. About 84% of the plants are in 14 families (out of the 44 listed). These are Buckwheat, Evening Primrose, Figwort, Four O'Clock, Lily, Mint, Mustard, Night-shade, Pea, Phlox, Poppy, Rose, Sunflower and Waterleaf. The serious wildflower-watcher may want to become familiar with the characteristics of these families so that flowers not listed in this book may more easily be identified.

5. Following the description is a line on which one might record when and where a particular wildflower was found. This could be a valuable record for future years. I have attempted to make this book small enough so that it is practical as a field manual and will add to your enjoyment as wildflower-watchers.

6. When looking at the Index of Common Names, please check the description first to find the name used under the photograph.

GLOSSARY

The following is a brief botanical glossary which hopefully will assist in understanding the descriptions of the flowers.

ANNUAL: A plant which goes from seed to maturity to death in one year.

ANTHER: The upper part of the stamen, which bears the pollen.

BARK: The outer tissue covering a stem, branch, or trunk.

BASAL: Usually refers to growth, such as leaves, at the base of a plant.

BELLY FLOWER: A plant less than 3 inches high. One that flower-watchers have to get down on their belly to appreciate.

BIENNIAL: A plant which goes from seed to maturity to death in two years.

BRACT: A small leaf under and part of the flower cluster.

BULB: An underground, onionlike unit usually with a husklike covering which, when moist, sends forth a plant.

CACTUS: Succulent, perennial plant with a large number of spines (thorns or stickers).

CALYX: The outer part of the flower, usually green, made up of sepals.

CATKIN: A dangling flower cluster or scaly spike as on Willows.

CHAPARRAL: Refers to the many different small-leaved evergreen shrubs with stiff or thorny branches which cover the foothills and mountains.

COROLLA: The inside part of the flower, made up of colored petals.

DECIDUOUS: A plant which loses its leaves, usually in the fall, and grows new leaves in the spring.

EVERGREEN: A plant which retains some leaves all year. Usually sheds leaves all year. Opposite of deciduous.

FLORET: A small, individual flower in a dense head or cluster of flowers.

FLOWER SPIKE: A long stem surrounded by individual flowers.

HERB: A plant without a visable woody base.

HOARY: A term given to plants covered with a white fuzz or down.

HYBRID: A plant which is the product of a cross of two species.

LEAF: A thin, expanded outgrowth of a plant stem or a twig, usually green, and consisting of a broad blade and stem. Leaves present a surface on which transpiration, respiration, and the absorption of light needed for the photosynthesis of food can occur.

LINEAR: Long and narrow, of uniform width.

MEMBRANACEOUS SHEATH: Thin, soft and pliable covering.

NODE: The joint of a stem; the point of insertion of a leaf or leaves.

OVARY: That part of the flower which develops the seed.

PERENNIAL: A plant which may originate from a seed, but which grows year after year. It may come back from its roots, or the part above the ground may be alive all year.

PETAL: A colored leaf which is part of the flower.

PISTIL: The seed-producing part of the flower. It includes the stigma and the ovary with a style in between.

POLLEN: The male spores. Found on the anther.

RACEME: A flower cluster in which the flowers are along a spike or stalk and the flower stems are of equal length.

RHIZOME: An underground stem or rootstock that produces leafy shoots on the upper side and roots on the underside.

SEED: Contains a miniature plant that is capable of developing independently into a plant similar to the one which produced it.

SEPAL: Leaflike parts that make up the outer part of the flower.

SHRUB: A smaller, perennial, woody plant, usually with a number of branches at the base.

SPINE: A stiff, sharp, pointed, woody body; similar to a thorn but smaller.

STALK: I use this nonbotanical term to describe the trunk or trunks of a plant.

STAMEN: The flower's male organ. It consists of a threadlike stem topped by the anther, which holds the pollen.

STEM: I use this term to describe the connecting link between the stalk and a leaf or the stalk and the flower. However, a flower or a leaf may have no stem and may grow directly from the stalk.

STIGMA: The top part of the pistil; where the pollen germinates.

STYLE: That part of the pistil between the stigma and the ovary.

SUCCULENT: Juicy, fleshy and soft.

TENDRIL: A slender coiling or twining organ by means of which a climbing plant grasps its support.

TREE: A large, perennial, woody plant with one or few main trunks.

UMBEL: A flowercluster shaped in the form of the supports of an umbrella where the stems come from a central point.

VINE: A plant with long runners, either over the ground or over supports.

WILDFLOWER: A very general term referring to all plants which may grow without benefit of human planting, cultivation and watering. This term includes plants which do not have flowers as commonly understood but which have catkins or other reproductive parts.

SPECTACULAR FIELDS OF
ANTELOPE VALLEY WILDFLOWERS

In years when the winter rains are average or above, the Antelope Valley is blessed with spectacular displays of colorful wildflowers that grow very close together in homogenous groupings and may cover many acres. For the neophyte or casual wildflower-watcher, knowing the names of these masses of flowers may initially be sufficient. To aid in identification, those wildflowers are listed below.

FLOWERS GROWING IN LARGE HOMOGENOUS GROUPS

YELLOW TO ORANGE: California Poppy, California Coreopsis, Bigelow Coreopsis, Goldfields, Desert Dandelion, Tidy Tips, Monolopia.

RED TO PURPLE: Desert Candle, Sand Verbena, Farewell to Spring, Red Stem Filaree, Owl's Clover.

BLUE TO LAVENDER: Royal Desert Lupine, Bush Lupine, Bentham Lupine, Pygmy Leaved Lupine, Chia, Thistle Sage, Davy Gilia.

WHITE TO CREAM: Cream Cups, Hoary Cress, Dune Primrose, Pennyroyal, Evening Snow, California Primrose.

FLOWERS GROWING IN SMALLER HOMOGENOUS GROUPS

YELLOW TO ORANGE: Desert Trumpet, Spencer Primrose, Pepper Grass, Hairy Lotus, Golden Gilia, Yellow Pincushion, Wallace Eriophyllum, Scale Bud.

RED TO PURPLE: Turkish Rugging, Red Ribbons, Fairy Trumpet, Chinese Houses, Crested Onion, Apricot Mallow, Mustang Clover.

BLUE TO LAVENDER: Parry Gilia, Lesser Gilia, Blue Mantle, Globe Gilia, Mesa Phlox, Chicory, Fremont Phacelia, Baby Blue Eyes.

WHITE TO CREAM: Forget-Me-Not, Brown Eyed Primrose, Wild Onion, White Lupine, Parry Gilia, Prickley Poppy, Miner's Lettuce.

I. PLANTS WITHOUT FLOWERS

A. CYPRESS FAMILY (Cupressaceae)
A family of trees or shrubs, many of which produce small, berrylike, woody cones on the ends of the branches. Pollen sacks form prior to cones.

California Juniper
Juniperus californica

Fls.: None. Fruit is a hard bluish berry or cone, about 1/2 inch in diameter, covered with white, powdery substance; some plants may have no berries while others nearby may be loaded with berries. **Ht.:** Bushy tree or shrub up to 20 feet. **Lvs.:** Short, round, dark-green, and scalelike, usually in whorls of three. **Areas:** Mostly on the west and south side of the Antelope Valley, usually growing among the Joshua Trees and the Great Basin Sage but sometimes in large stands with only small desert shrubs. Trunks have peeling bark,and,when the wood is cut a strong cedar smell is present. Indians ground the berries for food. They are eaten whole but not digested by coyotes. Plants vary, with fruit maturing to a reddish color in one, two, or three years.

Date_____Location_____

B. EPHEDRA OR JOINT FIR FAMILY (Ephedraceae)
Shrubs with jointed, reedlike stems. A very primitive family with 7 species in Southern Calif. all of which are similar to the one below.

Mormon Tea
(Indian Tea, Mexican Tea, Squaw Tea)
Ephedra californica

Fls.: Male plants have small, colorful, orange catkins (clusters of stamens) at the joints of the stems, while the female plant has small, green, scaly cones. Its long, jointed, reedy stems are the most noticeable feature about this shrub. **Ht.:** Usually less than 2 feet, but at times may reach 3 feet. **Lvs.:** Small, in whorls of three at joints which disappear soon after developing. **Areas:** Found in almost all areas including the foothills.

Indians, Mexicans and early pioneers used the plant to make a beverage which they felt relieved intestinal ailments. Indians would hang bunches of ephedra in alkali springs to improve the taste of the water.
Date_____Location_____

II. PETALS ABSENT OR NOT APPARENT

A. SPURGE FAMILY (Euphorbiaceae)
What look like flowers are really colored bracts (like a small leaf) that look like petals. Plants have a thick milky sap. The three-sided pistil is on a short stalk.

Rattlesnake Weed
(Sand Mat, Golondrina)
Euphorbia albomarginata
Fls.: Many very tiny, slightly cupped, round, white flowers with a maroon center. **Ht.:** A mat, barely 1/2 inch high; spreading from a perennial root with many branches; some up to 10 inches long. **Lvs.:** Round and green on reddish stems which have a milky sap. **Areas:** I,IV,VIII,X,XII,XIV. A very showy ground cover which got its common name, not from its appearance but, rather because at one time it was

thought to be useful as a treatment for snakebites. Jane Pinhiero calls it Golondrina and comments that it is "one of the commonest and yet most striking of these ground clinging matlike plants."
Date_____Location_____

B. GOOSEFOOT OR PIGWEED FAMILY (Chenopodiaceae)
The tiny flowers are made up of five or fewer sepals. The herbs are somewhat succulent and tend to be weedy. Both herbs and shrubs tend to grow on soils with high saline content.

Russian Thistle (alien)
(Tumbleweed)
Salsola iberica

Fls.: Tiny, made up of greenish or sometimes pink bracts, located throughout the plant from the base to the tips. **Ht.:** Up to 4 feet. **Lvs.:** First leaves are 1 inch or more long, narrow and pointed; the second set of leaves are short, awl-shaped, stiff and end in sharp points. **Areas:** Almost all, in soil that has previously been cultivated. Not a spring-blooming flower, but so common, it had to be included. Blooms in July and August. Seeds came to this country in 1873 or 1874 in flax seed that was planted in South Dakota. By 1895 it had infested 16 states and 13 Canadian provinces and has almost become a symbol of the West as the "tumbling tumbleweed." It probably came to the Antelope Valley in the early 1900s. A single plant can produce 20,000 to 50,000 seeds and when the wind breaks this dried, bushy plant off at the ground line and blows it across a field, one bush can reseed a considerable amount of land. In the middle 1960s, heavy rains followed by strong winds uprooted more than 100 acres of Russian Thistle and covered 32 blocks of Palmdale. Many front yards were covered from the curbs to the eves of the houses and "tumbleweeds" filled the backyards level with the tops of the walls.

Date_____Location_____

Hop Sage
Grayia spinosa

Fls.: Inconspicuous; noticeable because of the clusters of somewhat succulent green and rosy fruit at the ends of the branches on male plants. **Ht.:** 1 to 3 1/2 feet. **Lvs.:** Gray-green, somewhat fleshy, alternate on many branched, thorny limbs. **Areas:** I,II,III,IV,VI. Common on the desert floor. Eaten by grazing animals.

Date_____Location_____

Winter Fat
Eurotia lanata

Fls.: Not noticeable; notable feature of this erect shrub is the heavy, cottony appearance of the top one third of the plant. This plant should not be confused with the Cotton Thorn, which is completely covered with a cottony material after a heavy bloom of showy yellow flowers. **Lvs.:** Slightly wooly, lancelike, up to two inches long on white or grayish limbs. **Ht.:** 1 to 3 feet. **Areas:** IV. In some areas outside of the Antelope Valley, such as Nevada, Winter Fat may be the only shrub covering large areas and is an important winter grazing plant.

Date_____Location_____

C. CACAO FAMILY (Sterculiaceae)
This family is mostly made up of tropical plants. Only two are native to California and we have only one.

Fremontia
(Flannel Bush, Slippery Elm)
Fremontodendron californica

Fls.: Showy, 1 to 1 1/2 inches in diameter, 5 fleshy sepals (which can be mistaken for petals), orange or lemon yellow; 5 stamens branching from a single stem, alternate to the sepals; flowers are so thick on branches, most of the leaves are hidden. **Ht.:** Bushy tree or large shrub, up to 20 feet. **Lvs.:** Variable, 1/4 to 1 1/4 inches long, dark green with some fuzz on them, usually symmetrical, with a single notch on each side. **Areas:** Mainly in Big Rock Creek Canyon, Wrightwood and some in Pine Canyon. Blooms in May and June. Named for Capt. John C. Fremont, whose botanist discovered the plant. Hybridized by nursery-men for landscape plants. Used somewhat along freeways in the Los Angeles basin.

Date_____Location_____

D. BUCKWHEAT FAMILY (Polygonaceae)
Includes both herbs and low shrubs. Clusters of small flowers are made up of five or six colored, petal-like sepals (a leaflike flower part which ordinarily is beneath the petals). Swollen nodes. Leaves often have a membranaceous sheath where they attach to the stem. A large group of this family (Eriogonum) is noted for basal leaves.

Yellow Turban
Eriogonum pusillum

Fls.: Tiny, bright yellow to reddish on end of stems. **Ht.:** 4 to 12 inches. **Lvs.:** Basal, turning red with age. **Areas:** I,IV,XIII. Jane Pinheiro describes this plant as "a dainty, lacily branched bright green plant with a tiny puff of yellow blossoms at each stem... Under [a magnifying] glass one will find that what appear to be yellow puffs . . . are, in reality, clusters of five to thirty perfect minute blossoms."
Date_____Location_____

Desert Trumpet
Eriogonum inflatum

Fls.: Insignificant. **Ht.:** 8 to 32 inches. **Lvs.:** Basal. **Areas:** IV, VII,XII. Grows in colonies in foothills in clay soils, but solitary plants may be found in other soils. It is noticeable because of the inflated and hollow upper stalk. Looks like a skeleton.
Date_____Location_____

Wild Rhubarb
(Canaigre, Pie Plant)
Rumex hymenosepalus

Fls.: Many rust or pinkish sepals on a flower stalk. **Ht.:** 2 to 4 feet. **Lvs.:** Oblong, fleshy leaves up to 14 inches long growing from a smooth, reddish stalk. **Areas:** II,IV,VIII,XI,XIV. Similar to Rhubarb. Early settlers gathered stalks and canned them to be used in making pies. Roots are high in tannic acid. At one time an attempt was made to grow the plant commercially as a substitute for tanbark oak to provide tannic acid for tanning leather. This attempt was not successful because irrigation decreased the tannic acid from 25% to less than 5%. Leaves and roots are poisonous. Grows in sandy soil.
Date_____Location_____

Curly Dock
(Sour Dock)
Rumex crispus

Fls.: Dense clusters of tiny red flowers. **Ht.:** 2 to 4 feet. **Lvs.:** Basal, lancelike with curled edges. **Areas:** IV,VIII in moist meadows. Flower head much like the Wild Rhubarb, but narrower. Plants tend to grow close together.
Date_____Location_____

Turkish Rugging
(Turk's Rug)
Chorizanthe staticoides

Fls.: No petals, white and red brats in the forks of the branches. **Ht.:** 4 to 10 in. **Lvs.:** Basal, oblong. **Stems:** Reddish with many branches. **Areas:** IV,VIII,X. The common name is most appropriate because when they grow in large groups on the hills, they give the appearance of a beautiful red and white oriental carpet.
Date_____Location_____

Skeleton Weed
Eriogonum deflexum

Fls.: Tiny white flowers (turning pink with age) in pods hang from leafless branches. **Ht.:** 4 to 12 inches. **Lvs.:** Basal from which rises a single stalk which has many branches a few inches from the ground. **Areas:** IV,VIII.
Date_____Location_____

Punctured Bract
(Saucer Plant)
Oxytheca perfoliata

Fls.: Insignificant, white turning to pinkish, located above the large saucerlike bracts through which the stems pass. Stems and bracts are green turning to red with maturity. **Ht.:** 4 to 12 inches. **Lvs.:** Oblong at base of plant; **Areas:** I,II,III,IV. Plant is noticeable because of the deep red coloration and its unusual structure. A small blue butterfly lays its eggs on the plant and the larvae look like seeds at the bottom of the

saucerlike bracts. Jane Pinhiero comments, "In early summer, one comes upon patches of one of the strangest little plants of the desert. Except for several small greenish brown basal leaves and a tiny feathery tuft of white blossom, the entire plant is blood red. Its symmetrically branching stems pass through the centers of its three to five pointed leaves giving reason for the name Punctured Bract."
Date_____Location_____

California Buckwheat
(Wild Buckwheat)
Eriogonum fasciculatum ssp. polifolium
Fls.: Many very tiny, white flowers with pink centers in a tight pod which turns to rusty red as the flowers mature, many pods on each shrub. **Ht.:** 1 to 3 feet high and sometimes 2 to 4 feet in diameter. **Lvs.:** 1 inch long, tapering at both ends, growing in clusters up the slender, flexible branches; evergreen. **Areas:** One of the most common shrubs in Southern California. It can be found in great numbers throughout the foothills surrounding the Valley. One cannot appreciate the beauty of these flowers without looking at the pods with a magnifying glass or at least through a macro lens on a single lens reflex camera. Extensively used as a bee plant, but is not the plant from which buckwheat flour is made.
Date_____Location_____

Flattop Buckwheat
Eriogonum plumatella
Fls.: Tiny, white, in clusters on top of an erect shrub in kind of a platform or flattop. **Ht.:** 1 to 3 feet. **Lvs.:** Grayish, sparse, lancelike on very crooked and many-branched limbs, woody at the base. **Areas:** IV. Even when this shrub is not blooming, it is easy to pick out because of the skeletonlike appearance and the flattop.
Date_____Location_____

III. Petals: 3, 6 or 9

A. LILY FAMILY (Liliaceae)
Petals and sepals in patterns of three's (3, 6 or 9) and colored much the same. Either 3 or 6 stamens. The plant grows from bulbs, some of which are poisonous. Leaves are usually long and narrow, but may sometimes be sword-shaped.

Golden Mariposa Lily
(Club-Haired Mariposa Tulip)
Calochortus clavatus

Fls.: Showy, 3 petals, lemon yellow with ragged rust line near bottom of petals, 6 purple anthers. **Ht.:** 12 to 24 inchs. **Lvs.:** Long and narrow, grow from base and where branched. **Areas:** VII,IX. Found in colonies in the foothills in soil of serpentine origin. These flowers bloom only when there is sufficient winter rain or snow to penetrate the soil deep enough to provide moisture to their bulbs. This is one of many of the Butterfly Tulips (as the Spanish called them) which grow in the area. Indians harvested bulbs of the many species of Calochortus for food and in such a manner so as to promote their multiplication. In 1887 one nurseryman shipped a quarter of a million of these lily bulbs (all collected in the wild) to England to be planted in English gardens.
Date_____Location_____

Desert Mariposa
Calochortus kennedyi

Fls.: Bowl-shaped, reddish orange petals. **Ht.:** 2 to 14 in. (depending upon whether it is in the open or trying to reach the sun through a desert shrub). **Lvs.:** Long, narrow, curling. **Areas:** II,III,IV. Plants grow from a bulb but seldom grow close together. In Spanish, mariposa means butterfly, and the name came from the markings on the petals. There are a number of other red or purple species of Calochortus both on the desert floor and in the canyons, especially in Bouquet Canyon. These are all very similar as to the shape of the flower and leaves, but vary in color and in the markings at the base of the petals.
Date_____Location_____

Palmer Primrose
Calochortus palmeri

Fls.: 3 bowl shaped, rose to reddish-brown petals, hairy at the base. **Ht.:** 4 to 12 inches. **Lvs.:** Long, narrow, curling. **Areas:** VI. Grows in moist, alkaline soil. At one time, these were plentiful on 10th St. West, Ave I and 20th St. West in Lancaster, but most of this area is now covered with houses. However in a rainy year they still may be found.
Date_____Location_____

White Mariposa
Calochortus venustus

Fls.: 3 white (sometimes pale rose or lilac), bowl-shaped petals, 1 to 1 3/4 inches broad and 1 to 2 1/2 inches long; has a reddish-brown spot two thirds of the way down the petal, under which are reddish-brown markings. **Ht.:** 2 to 3 feet. **Lvs.:** Narrow, long, basal leaves. **Areas:** IX,X. Grows from a bulb.
Date_____Location_____

Desert Zygadene
Zigadenus brevibracteatus

Fls.: Clusters of 6-petaled flowers, about 1 inch in diameter develop at the ends of the many branches growing from a single stalk. **Ht.:** 12 to 20 inches. **Lvs.:** Few, long and straplike at base of stalk. **Areas:** III. Plant grows from a bulb and is similar to the Death Camas, which is extremely poisonous. It is believed that all species of this genus are toxic in varying degrees. Many years, these plants are not seen at all. However, in years when there is plenty of rain, they are numerous in Hi Vista.
Date_____Location_____

Soap Plant
(Wavy Leaved Soap Plant, Amole)
Chlorogalum pomeridianum

Fls.: Small, elongated, bluish-green buds open into what appears to be a 6-petaled (actually 3 are sepals), white, 1 inch flower. The flowers bloom in small clusters on long, thin branches for 4 to 6 hours each evening (between 6:00P.M. and midnight). Petals are separate and curling with a greenish midvein. Clusters begin blooming at the bottom of the branch, bloom for one evening and then go to seed. The next evening the cluster above will bloom. It takes roughly two weeks to bloom from the bottom of the branch to the top. **Ht.:** Up to 8 1/2 feet with 5 to 9 branches beginning at least one third of the way up the stalk. **Lvs.:** Basal, wavy, up to 2 feet long, mostly dried by time of bloom. **Areas:** IV,IX. The 4 to 6 inch blubs are covered with a brown husk. Indians and early pioneers had many uses for the bulbs: husks for bed ticking; crushed bulb as a soap for cleaning clothes and baskets and for poisoning fish in streams; whole blub roasted like a potato. (Roasting removed the poison.) Many of these plants grow in the foothills but are seldom seen because of the time of bloom.

Date_____Location_____

B. AMARYLLIS FAMILY (Amaryllidaceae)
Three or 6 petals. The flowers are on the end of leafless stalks, many times in the form of an umbel. A single bract usually occurs at the central point.

Golden Stars
Bloomeria crocea

Fls.: Yellow, 6 petals, many blooms in an umbel at the top of a single, smooth, naked, stalk. **Ht.:** 6 to 14 inches. **Lvs.:** Basal, strap, but not noticeable when flower is in bloom. **Areas:** XIII, XV. Look for colonies of these showy flowers in late spring just off of Highway 138 as the road enters the western foothills.

Date_____Location_____

Fringed Onion
Allium fimbriatum

Fls.: Many rose to purple flowers in a small flower head on the end of a weak, smooth stem. **Ht.:** From lying on the ground to maybe 4 inches. **Lvs.** Usually one long, narrow, curling strap leaf. **Areas:** III,IV. In moderately sized groups. If it smells like an onion, it must be an onion.

Date_____Location_____

Crested Onion
Allium fimbriatum mohavense

Fls.: Many white flowers with pinkish midveins in a small umbel at the end of a smooth, weak stem. **Ht.:** 3 to 8 inches. **Lvs.:** Single strap leaf growing from the base. **Areas:** VII and in the Ana Verde Valley as well as on the north side of Ave. S near the Palmdale Hospital. Usually grows in moderately sized groups. Has a strong onion or garlic odor.
Date_____Location_____

Blue Dicks
(Brodiaea, Wild Hyacinth)
Dichelostemma pulchella

Fls.: Several tiny 6-petaled flowers in a compact ball at top of a reedy, naked stem. **Ht.:** 1 to 2 feet. **Lvs.:** One or two long, narrow strap leaves at base. **Areas:** I,VII,VIII,X,XI,XII,XIII. Tends to grow in small groups among other plants. Grows from a small corm, about 6 inches below the earth's surface. One common name is Brodiaea because the botanical name was once Brodiaea.
Date_____Location_____

C. AGAVE FAMILY (Agavaceae)
Noted for their sharp, rigid, spearlike "leaves." Drought resistant as it has a rhizome or an underground stem or rootstock. Only two species (Yucca and Joshua Tree) are native to the Antelope Valley.

Joshua Tree
(Yucca Palm, Tree Yucca)
Yucca brevifolia

Fls.: Many 6-petaled, creamy white flowers with greenish tints and streaks of rust colors, in a large head (measuring up to 18 inches long) at ends of branches. The flower head begins as a rocket shaped bud wrapped in heavily textured and colorful leaflike brats. As the head develops, flowers appear, followed by seed pods extending from the center of each flower. At maturity, the stalk at the end of the limbs holds many 2 to 3-inch seedpods, which fall or are knocked off and are eaten by birds and rodents. The seeds look like watermelon seeds. **Ht.:** 8 to 30 feet, depending greatly on where the tree grows. Ones near Gorman are very short while ones around Wilsona may exceed 30 feet, (the record of which I am aware is 54 feet). **Lvs.:** rigid, narrow, spiney, green with brown needle-like tips, less than 12 inches long, (which gives the plant the botanical name, brevifolia, because the leaves are shorter than other Yucca), as the leaves die, they turn brownish gray and form a mat against the trunk, later falling off leaving a pock marked bark; **Areas:** all of the area, with the western most along Highway 5 in Hungry Valley near Gorman, extending to over 6000 feet near Big Bear and up into Nevada and Utah as well as down near Indio. Bloom is very irregular. In 1985 after heavy, long lasting snows, it seemed like every branch had a flower head, but in 1986 after normal rains and snow almost no flower heads could be found.

Date_____Location_____

Joshua Tree Folklore

"Associated with the idea of barren sands, their stiff and ungraceful form makes them to the traveler the most repulsive tree in the vegetable kingdom". So wrote Capt. John C. Fremont after seeing these "Yucca Palms" while crossing the western end of Antelope Valley in 1844. Mormon pioneers going from San Bernardino to Salt Lake City are credited with naming the Joshua Tree after the prophet in the old testament who raised his arms pointing the way to the promised land. In their case so did the Joshua Tree. The name "Yucca Palms" apparently came from Fremont's and other early explorers belief that they were related to the "yucca" (also called cassava or manihot) a plant in South America from which comes tapioca. Actually, the two are in entirely different families.

Joshua Trees (Yucca brevifolia and Y. brevifolia var. jaegeriana) are confined to the Mojave Desert, northwestern Arizona, southwestern Utah and parts of Nevada. It is only a myth that they also grow in the Palestine. Because of the six petaled flowers and the large bulbs growing several feet under the tree, botanists originally placed the plant in the Lily Family. A botanical reorganization has now placed them in the Agave Family. Because of the lack of growth rings in the fibrous trunk it is impossible to determine the age of any one tree. Some botanists have estimated that some trees may live to be 800 to 900 years old. Based on observations of the formation of "petrified yucca" in the living tree, this writer believes that the trees probably live much longer than 1000 years. Edmund C. Jaeger in his book "The California Deserts" says, "The so-called petrified wood, much prized as fuel by desert settlers, is made by the plant as it lays down silica in the cell walls in its attempt to walloff the injuries done by the borers, by fire, or by wind". The word "petrified" is obviously a misnomer because the material burns like coal unlike the fibrous part of the tree. (As a boy, the writer had much experience in picking up petrified wood to burn *in our home cookstove.)* Fossil remains and dung of the extinct giant ground sloth indicate that various species of yucca were the primary food for this and other prehistoric animals.

The Panamint Indians ate the young flower buds immediately after roasting them over hot coals. They are high in carbohydrates and very nutritious. In the 1880s an English firm cut many Joshua Trees, hauled them to the pulp mill at Ravenna (east of Acton) and then to England where they attempted to make paper. Fortunately poor quality paper and high cost halted that operation. During World War I the wood was used to manufacture surgeons' splints and artificial limbs.

The Joshua Tree and the dead material which tends to build up around the base of mature trees are home to many insects, birds and small animals. There is a symbiotic relationship between the pronuba moth and the yuccas. Each depends on the other for pollenation and procreation. The Yucca Night Lizard is entirely dependant on the yuccas and cannot live without them.

Yucca
(Our Lord's Candle, Our Lord's Candlestick, Whipple Yucca, Quixote Plant, Quiote)
Yucca whipplei

Fls.: hundreds of creamy white, 6 petaled flowers, 1 to 1 1/2 inches in diameter on the upper third to one half of a green stalk, sometimes flowers appear to be in a spiral up the stalk; **Ht.:** 6 to 14 feet; **Lvs.:** rigid, narrow, spiney, green with brown needle-like tips, up to 30 inches long, radiating in all directions from the base; **Areas;** IV, V, VII, VIII, IX, X, XIV, XV. This plant is neither a tree, shrub, or cacti but rather a salspitosi or woody perennial. After the seeds mature the entire plant including the leaves at the base dies. The following year a new plant comes from the stolens (roots) or from seed but may not bloom for several more years. The new stalk is reddish and resembles an oversize asparagus stalk and may grow 6 inches each day. It turns green as flower buds sprout. The Yucca which grows in the higher mountains and along the southern base of the San Gabriel Mountains is a different subspecies and is noted by a much larger trunk than the ones north of the Mountains.

Date_____Location_____

Yucca Folklore

To the Indian, the Yucca was a veritable supermarket. The leaves and the roots when pounded provided a very effective, green soap. Fiber obtained from the dead leaves was used to make a remarkably strong cordage, woven into mats, baskets and loin cloths as well as ceremonial costumes. The color of the fibers varied with the species and the soil upon which the plant grew. Paint brushes were made from the base of the leaves for painting the face and body and of course the sharp points of the leaves were used for needles.

Immature green stalks have a high sugar content and were used by some tribes to make an alcoholic beverage. Some tribes warmed the stalks, pounded them, steeped them in water and drank the water as a laxative. Stalks could also be barbecued by cooking slowly in a fire pit much like cooking potatoes. Tender stalks were eaten raw or dried for later consumption. However, stalks reaching the bud stage are poisonous and were avoided. (The writer can verify this from personal experience, when as a boy hiking in the foothills above Palmdale, he mistakenly choose to try to quench his thirst by eating the meat of a more mature green yucca stalk. It was sweet; the more I ate, the more I wanted. The result was severe dehydration and a very sick little boy.)

The blossoms were cooked as a vegetable in watertight woven baskets by placing heated rocks in water covering the blossoms and stirring constantly so the rocks did not damage the baskets. Seeds were gathered while still green and ripened in the sun. Ripe seeds were eaten either raw, boiled or after being roasted over hot coals. Seeds were also ground into a meal, worked into a paste and spread on mats or flat rocks to dry. The cake was later reworked and finally formed into blocks and dried again. They were stored for winter food or used to barter with other tribes.

Dr. Bigelow with the Whipple expedition in the early 1800s first recorded the discovery of the plant in the San Bernardino Valley and Cajon Pass. Although there many plants named after Dr. Bigelow, it was left to another botanist, Dr. John Torrey to give the plant it's botanical name after the leader of the previous named expedition. The very descriptive name "Our Lord's Candle" has been used at least since 1882 when Jeanne C. Carr (John Muir's friend) used it in an article in the "California Magazine" and may have come from one of the Spanish names for the plant, "Lampara de Dios" (Lamp of God). The Navajo name for the species of yucca growing in Arizona is "yaybi-tsa-si" which literally mean "yucca of the gods". Whatever the source, it very nicely meets both the poetic and graphic requirements for a common name.

As with the Joshua Tree, there is an interesting symbiotic relationship between the yuccas and the Pronuba Moth. Although the yuccas may be pollinated by other insects, the Pronuba moth is the main pollinator. As for the moth, it is solely dependant on the yuccas to provide an environment for its life cycle.

IV. PETALS: 4 or 6

A. POPPY FAMILY (Papaveraceae)

4 or 6 (rarely 8) separate, showy petals. Many stamens. Sepals fall off when flower opens. Herbs and shrubs have yellow or milky sap.

California Poppy

Eschscholtzia californica

Fls.: 4 Petals, (sometimes 6 or 8), deep orange to yellow to white and variegated. **Ht.:** 6 to 18 inches. **Lvs.:** Lacy, fernlike, gray-green. **Areas:** VIII,X,XV with the most spectacular fields in XI,XII and XIV. An exceedingly variable plant in growth and color. Dr. Philip Munz indicates that there are some 50 subspecies but does not name any of them. In the Antelope Valley we have perennials, biennials and annuals as well as many different colors. It was hoped that when the California Poppy Re-serve was established, a much-needed, intensive study of the flower would be made. Eschscholtzias are distinguished by the orange ring at the base of the petals where the calyx or cap was attached. It must fall off before the petals can untwist and open.

Date_____Location_____

California Poppy Folklore

La Sabanilla de San Pasqual (The Altar-cloth of St. Pascal) is the name Spanish sailors gave to the glorious fields of poppies which blanketed the California shores in the late 1700s. They were referring to the shepherd saint who tended his flock far from church and village and knelt in fields of wildflowers to commune with God. It seems to be no coincidence that the area in which the most spectacular fields of poppies grew, came to be known as Rancho San Pasqual. This area is now known as Pasadena, Altadena and Sierra Madre.

Other names for the California Poppy have been *Copa De Ora* (Cup of Gold), *Amapola, Torosa and Dormidera* (meaning the sleepy ones, for the flowers close up at night and when it is cloudy or when the wind blows). The vast fields of poppies were also called *La Tierra Del Fuego* (The Land of Fire). The botanical name Eschscholtzia was given to the plant by poet-naturalist Adelbert Von Chamisso of the Fussian scientific expedition headed by Otto von Kotzebue, who visited California in 1816. The name honored his lifelong friend and surgeon on the ship, Dr. Johann Friedrich Eschscholtz.

The California Poppy was designated the state flower in 1903. This was an easy and excellent choice since this spectacular flower is indigenous only to California and small parts of Oregon and Arizona. However, because of the widespread exportation of seed and the plant's tendency to escape from cultivation when the climatic conditions are correct, fields of California Poppies may now be seen in India and parts of Australia.

Indians used the fresh roots as a toothache remedy since they are slightly narcotic. An extract was used as a liniment to relieve headaches and some Indians cooked the foliage as a vegetable. The Luisenos Indians near San Diego chewed the petals like chewing gum. The early Spanish were convinced that poppies would make hair grow. The petals were mixed with olive oil or suet, cooked over a slow fire and strained. The result was *Pomada de Amapola* which was faithfully rubbed onto balding heads.

Little Gold Poppy
Eschscholtzia minutiflora

Fls.: 4-petaled, orange. **Ht.:** 1 to 3 inches. **Lvs.:** Lacy, fernlike, gray-green. **Areas:** I. You have to look closely to spot this miniature version of the California Poppy. Grows early in the season with the Coreopsis and Monolopia off of Bacchus Road.
Date_____Location_____

Golden Ear Drops
Dicentra chrysantha

Fls.: Yellow clusters of flowers resembling a pair of upside down golden ear bobs grow at the end of stems growing out of the top third of the main stalk. **Ht.:** Up to 6 feet. **Lvs.:** Lacy, fernlike, gray-green (much like the Calif. Poppy), mostly at the base of the stalks. **Areas:** IV,IX.X. Large solitary plants or in large bunches. This is one of those plants which confuses botanists as well as us common flower-watchers in that the flower is similar to those in the Bleeding Heart family, where it was listed for some time, but the foliage is like some flowers in the Poppy family, where it is presently listed.
Date_____Location_____

Prickly Poppy
Argemone corymbosa

Fls.: 6 crepe paperlike, very white petals measuring 2 to 3 1/2 inches across with many prominent yellow stamens. **Ht.:** 2 to 5 feet. **Lvs.:** Large, deeply lobed, leathery stalk; leaves and buds are covered with sharp thorns. **Areas:** IV,V,VIII,X,XI,XII,XIV. Grows in small colonies over a widespread area. Seeds are highly narcotic but it would take many acres of the plant to make it feasible for anyone to harvest the seed for its narcotic quality. The flower is very similar to the Matilija Poppy, which makes a far better landscape shrub than does this one.
Date_____Location_____

Cream Cups
Platystemon californicus

Fls.: 6 creamy white petals, sometimes streaked butter yellow, many stamens. **Ht.:** 4 to 12 inches. **Lvs.:** Long, narrow at base, long stems are covered with fine hairs. **Areas:** I,X,XI,XII,XIII,XIV. May be found in large groupings throughout the western part of the Antelope Valley. They are most attractive when found mixed with the California Poppy.
Date_____Location_____

Bush Poppy
(Tree Poppy)
Dendromecon rigida

Fls.: Showy, golden yellow, 1 to 3 inches across, 4 petals, many stamens with orange anthers often completely covering the shrub; seedpod similar to but smaller than the California Poppy. **Ht.:** Up to 8 feet. **Lvs.:** Blue-green, leathery, long and pointed, tending to point upward. **Areas:** IX,X. May have scattered growth in chaparral or may be found in great masses after a fire until gradually crowded out by other shrubs. This is such an attractive shrub that David Douglas, seed collector for the Royal Horticultural Society of London in the first quarter of the nineteenth-century, had hoped to domesticate it in English gardens but he had little success. However, in the local areas it is a nice landscape shrub.
Date_____Location_____

V. PETALS: 4 OR 5

A. BUCKTHORN FAMILY (Rhamnaceae)
A family of shrubs and small trees (sometimes climbers) that are most often quite thorny. Four or five stamens are opposite the petals.

Mountain Lilac
(California Lilac, Chaparral Whitethorn, Soap Bush)
Ceanothus leucodermis

Fls.: Showy, fragrant, light to dark blue; tiny 5-petal florets in a head much like the domestic lilac usually cover the shrub in great profusion; heads 1 to 3 inches long. **Ht.:** 5 to 12 feet. **Lvs.:** Heart-shaped to oval, blue-green to green, alternate and evergreen on thorny, gray to white branches. **Areas:** V,VII,IX,X,XIV. There are some 60 species of Ceanothus, 40 of which are native to California. Hybridizes easily both in the wild and in nurseries so that enormous veriation is found. Some of these hybrids are found along the freeways in the Los Angeles basin and are excellent landscape shrubs in a large yard. The flowers of most Ceanothus produce an abundant amount of cleansing lather when rubbed together in water. Leaves, bark and seeds also produce lather, but less abundantly. Because of this quality, a great many Ceanothus may be referred to as a Soap Bush. Ceanothus comes from the Greek word Keanothus, referring to a prickly plant. Most do have thorns.
Date_____Location_____

Buckbrush
Ceanothus cuneatus

Fls.: Tiny clusters of white, light lavender or sometimes light blue on umbels which, at the height of the blooming season, cover the shrub. **Ht.:** 3 to 8 feet. **Lvs.:** Opposite, evergreen, heavily-veined, elliptical with blunt, rounded ends, 1/4 to 1 inch long. **Areas:** IV,V,VII,X. One of the most common of the Ceanothus throughout California. However the most likely location in our area is in Big Rock Creek Canyon. Brush fires help seeds germinate so that in many places, large thickets of Buckbrush often grow on burned areas. (Please note: There is no photograph in the pictorial section.)
Date_____Location_____

Deerbrush
Ceanothus integerrimus
Fls.: White to dark blue or
pink; long, loose flower
clusters at ends of light
green or yellowish, droop-

ing branches. **Ht.:** 3 to 12 feet. **Lvs.:** Alternate, semi-deciduous or deciduous, elliptical with either rounded or pointed tips. **Areas:** V,VII,X. Most likely area is in Pine Canyon.
Date_____Location_____

B. TAMARISK FAMILY (Tamaricaceae)
Small trees or bushy shrubs which tend to grow on alkaline soils. The family contains both evergreen and deciduous plants. After the deciduous plants leaf out, they look the same as the evergreen plants.

Smallflower Tamarisk   (alien)
Tamarix parviflora
Fls.: Plant is deciduous; showy, rust-colored buds cover whiplike branches before leaves appear; pink, dainty, 4-petaled flowers are very fragrant. **Ht.:** Small tree or shrub, 10 to 18 feet. **Lvs.:** Gray-green, cordlike leaves up to 4 inches, salty to the taste. **Areas:** Notably area VIII. These trees were imported and planted as windbreaks or to control erosion, but have been found to be a most inappropriate plant for the desert region because of the inordinate amount of water they remove from use by native plants.
Date_____Location_____

French Tamarisk   (alien)
(Salt Cedar)
Tamarix gallica
Fls.: Bunches of wispy, 5-petaled pink and white flowers. **Ht.:** Up to 20 feet. **Lvs.:** Gray-green, cordlike leaves up to 4 inches, salty to the taste, evergreen. **Areas:** Widespread over desert floor, planted as windbreaks. Some have escaped from cultivation or linger on old homestead sites. Inappropriate for desert regions because of amount of moisture removed from use by native plants. May freeze back to roots in coldest winters.
Date_____Location_____

C. BUCKEYE FAMILY (Hippocastanaceae)

Trees and shrubs with opposite palmate leaves. Only one species listed here.

California Buckeye
(Horse Chestnut)
Aesculus californica

Fls.: Small, pinkish-white or rose, 4 petals, 5 to 7 stamens with orange tips (anthers) surround erect, 6 to 10 inch long spikes at ends of branches. Very showy in that the spikes cover the entire tree. **Ht.:** Bushy tree, 10 to 40 feet. **Lvs.:** Large, palmate, light green. **Areas:** X. Notably in Pine Canyon and on Lake Hughes Rd. Blooms in early June and goes dormant in August. The large seed-pods were used by Indians to poison streams and lakes to catch fish and were also processed to eliminate the poison so they could be eaten.

Date_____Location_____

VI. PETALS: 4

A. MUSTARD FAMILY (Cruciferae)

This very large family contains many of our table vegetables, such as radishes, broccoli, turnips, cabbage, and mustard greens. The flowers are a regular maltese cross shape with 4 petals and sepals of equal length. The family's characteristic 4 long and 2 short stamens make it easy to identify.

Pepper Grass
Lepidium flavum

Fls.: Yellow clusters of tiny 4-petaled flowers grow at the ends of branches. **Ht.:** 2 to 3 inches. **Lvs.:** Long, narrow, notched. **Areas:** II and III in the early season. Not a grass at all, but rather many plants grouped together, causing the appearance of a ground cover. Leaves are spicy to taste, from whence comes the common name. To appreciate this plant, one must walk out into the desert because masses of them can be hidden by the desert shrubs.

Date_____Location_____

Western Wallflower
Erysimum capitatum

Fls.: Bright yellow (sometimes orange), 4 petals in domed clusters at the ends of stout stalks which may or may not branch out from the base. The center stalk is the tallest. **Ht.:** 12 to 40 inches. **Lvs.:** Long, narrow, growing up stalk to just under the cluster of flowers. **Areas:** Widespread throughout the area with particularly good stands in Bouquet Canyon (Area IV), on Three Points Road and on Valyermo Road. At one time, many of these could be seen on vacant lots in Lancaster. The common name comes from a similar species growing next to and out of walls in England. Used extensively in England as a landscaping plant. Could be used here in landscaping because it has a rather long blooming period. However, the flowers become somewhat ragged at the end of bloom.
Date_____Location_____

Tumble Mustard   (alien)
Sisymbrium altissimum

Fls.: Typical yellow "mustard flowers" with 4 separate petals and 6 stamens (4 long and 2 short) blooming at the top of and at the ends of branches coming from a very sturdy stalk. **Ht.:** 2 to 3 feet. **Lvs.:** Large, lobed, dark green, mostly on lower part of plant. **Areas:** Most. When the Tumble Mustard dries, it forms a very sturdy but brittle skeleton that is frequently uprooted by the winds and blown tumbling across the fields, piling up against fences. There are a number of other mustards which are very similar except they do not have a heavy skeleton when dry and the leaves vary. Two common roadside mustards are Field Mustard, Brassica rapa, and Black Mustard, Brassica nigra, which may grow more than 10 feet high in wet years. All three of these as well as similar mustards growing on the Coast were brought here by the Spanish mission fathers by way of Mexico. The seeds of several species were ground to make table mustard, and the tender leaves were cooked as a potherb. The only native mustard is the Tansy Mustard (Descurainia pinnata), which has lacy leaves on the lower part of the stalk. Seeds of the native mustard were ground by the Indians and used in their pinole (mush).
Date_____Location_____

1   Goldfields   p.140

2   Dune Primrose   p.104

3   California Coreopsis   p.141

4   Yellow Turban   p.16

5 Desert Trumpet p.16

6 Golden Mariposa p.19

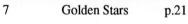

7   Golden Stars   p.21

8   California Poppy   p.26

9   Little Gold Poppy   p.27

10   Golden Ear Drops   p.27

11   Cream Cups   p.28

12   Pepper Grass   p.31

13   Tumble Mustard   p.32

14   Western Wallflower   p.32

15   Prince's Plume   p.96

16   Slender Keel Fruit   p.96

17   Spencer Primrose   p.102

18   Mustard-Like Primrose p.102

19   Desert Suncups   p.102

20   Lg. Yllw Desert Primrose   p.103

21   Hooker Primrose   p.103

22   Hairy Lotus   p.106

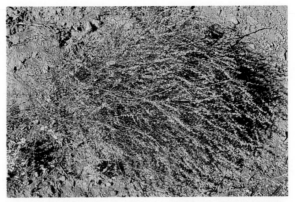

23   Broom Deer Weed   p.106

24   Loco Weed   p.106

25   Giant Blazing Star   p.118

26   Comet Blazing Star   p.117

27   Johnny Jump-Up   p.110

28   Wild Parsley   p.118

29   Apricot Mallow   p.111

30   Yellow Paintbrush   p.122

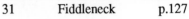

31   Fiddleneck   p.127

33   Golden Gilia   p.133

32   Whispering Bells   p.129

34   Common Monkey Flower   p.123

35   Common Sunflower   p.140

36   Goldfields   p.140

37   Bigelow Coreopsis   p.141

38   California Coreopsis   p.141

39   Monolopia   p.141

40   Yellow Pincushion   p.143

41   **Balsam Root**   p.142

42   **Tidy Tips**   p.142

43   **Wallace Eriophyllum**   p.143

44   Golden Yarrow   p.144

45   Desert Dandelion   p.144

46   Scale Bud   p.145

47   Silver Puff   p.145

48   Autumn Vinegar Weed p.144

49   Live Forever   p.115

50   Russian Thistle   p.14

51   Wild Rhubarb   p.16

52   Punctured Bract   p.17

53   Curly Dock   p.17

54   Turkish Rugging   p.17

56   Desert Mariposa   p.19

55   Scarlet Larkspur   p.113

58   Desert Candle   p.97

57   Palmer Mariposa   p.20

59   Fringed Onion   p.21

60   Sand Verbena   p.100

61   Wishbone Bush   p.101

62   Jewel Flower   p.96

63   Rock Cress   p.97

64   Wine Cups   p.103

65   Giant 4 O'Clock   p.100

66   Red Ribbons   p.104

67   Farewell-to-Spring   p.104

68   Desert Rattleweed   p.107

69   Red Maids   p.110

70   Elegant Lupine   p.108

71   Pin-Point Clover   p.107

72   Birdsfoot Trefoil   p.107

73   Checker Bloom   p.111

74   Indian Pinks   p.116

75   Wooly Paintbrush   p.122

76   Indian Paintbrush   p.122

77   Owl's Clover   p.123

79   Fairy Trumpet   p.124

78   Scarlet Bugler   p.125

80   Rosy Milkweed   p.126

81   Red Stem Filaree   p.112

82   Beard-tongue   p.125

83   Purple Mat   p.129

84   Desert Calico   p.131

85   Mustang Clover   p.131

86   Desert Straw   p.146

87   Mojave Thistle   p.147

Blue to Lavender

88   Blue Dicks   p.22

89   Lupine   p.108

90   Royal Desert Lupine   p.108

91   Pygmy-Leaved Lupine   p.109

92   Bentham Lupine   p.109

93   Bush Lupine   p.109

94   Parish Larkspur   p.113   95   Chia   p.119

96   Thistle Sage   p.119   97   Chinese Houses   p.124

98   Pine Penstemon   p.125

99   Lacy Phacelia   p.129

100   Davy Gilia   p.132

101   Globe Gilia   p.132

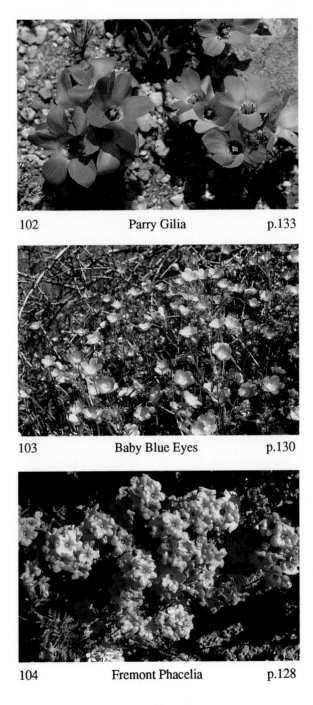

102   Parry Gilia   p.133

103   Baby Blue Eyes   p.130

104   Fremont Phacelia   p.128

105   Purple Nightshade   p.136

106   Blue Mantle   p.133

107   Mesa Phlox   p.134

108   Mojave Aster   p.146

White to Cream

110   Desert Zygadene   p.20

111   Soap Plant   p.20

112   Rattlesnake Weed   p.13

113   Skeleton Weed   p.17

114   White Mariposa   p.20

115   Crested Onion   p.22

116   Prickly Poppy   p.28

117   Cream Cups   p.28

118   Spectacle Pod   p.97

119   Shield Cress   p. 99

120   Hoary Cress   p.98

121   Woody Bottlewasher   p.105

122   Dune Primrose   p.104

123   California Primrose   p.105

124   Brown-Eyed Primrose   p.105

125   Water Cress   p.98

126   Giant 4 O'Clock   p.100

127   White Lupine   p.110

128   White Sage   p.120

129   Miner's Lettuce   p.110

130   Pennyroyal   p.120

131   Western Forget-Me-Not   p.128

132   Horehound   p.120

133   Desert Tobacco   p.136

135   Chinese Pusley   p.128

134   Forget-Me-Not   p.127

136   Parry Gilia   p.133

137   Evening Snow   p.134

138   Narrow Leaved Milkweed   p.126

139   Desert Milkweed   p.126

140   Yerba Mansa   p.139

141   Desert Tidy Tips   p.142

142   Fremont Pincushion   p.143

143   Silver Puff   p.145

144   Pearly Everlasting   p.147

146   Fremontia   p.15

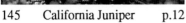

145   California Juniper   p.12

147   Joshua Tree   p.22

148   Joshua Tree Bud   p.22

149   Joshua Tree Flower Head   p.22

150   Joshua Tree Flower   p.22

151   Yucca   p.24

152   Yucca, Immature Stalk   p.24

153   Yucca Buds   p.24

154   Yucca Buds   p.24

155   Yucca Blossoms   p.24

156 Small Flower Tamarisk p.30

157   French Tamarisk   p.30

158   Elderberry Tree   p.139

159   Mormon Tea   p.12

160   California Buckeye   p.31

161   Winter Fat   p.15

162   California Buckwheat   p.18

163   Field of California Poppies

Western Antelope Valley

164   Hop Sage   p.14

165   Flattop Buckwheat   p.18

166   Bush Poppy   p.28

167   Mountain Lilac   p.29

168   DeerBrush   p.30

169   Desert Alyssum   p.99

170   Bladder Pod   p.99

171   Blue Sage   p.121

172   Bedstraw   p.101

173   Poison Oak   p.115

174   Bush Mallow   p.111   175   Creosote Bush   p.112

176   Squaw Bush   p.114

177   Chamise   p.117

178   Cliffrose   p.116

179   California Wild Rose   p.116

180   Paper Bag Bush   p.121

181   Bush Monkey Flower   p.123

182   Whorl-Leaf Penstemon   p.125

183   Wooly Blue Curls   p.121

184   Poodle Dog Bush   p.131

185   Jimson Weed   p.137

186   Great Basin Sage   p.149

187   Thickleaf Yerba Santa   p.130

188   Sticky-leaved Yerba Santa   p.130

189   Bigberry Manzanita   p.136

190   Anderson Thorn   p.137

191   Peach Thorn   p.137

192   Brittlebush   p.147

193   Linear Leafed Goldenbush   p.148

194   Cooper Goldenbush   p.148

195   Bindweed   p.135

196   Cotton Thorn   p.148

197   Cotton Thorn in Seed   p.148

198   California Dodder   p.135

199   Calabazilla   p.138

200   Clematis   p.114

201   Clematis in Seed   p.114

202   Wild Cucumber   p.138

203   Silver Cholla   p.149

204   Beavertail Cactus   p.149

205   Calif. Poppies and Cream Cups   p.26 , 28

206   California Poppies   p.26

207   Tidy Tips (two toned)   p.142

Prince's Plume
(Desert Plume)
Stanleya pinnata

Fls.: Many tiny, long, linear, yellow petals with 6 stamens (4 long and 2 short) form a flower spike, blooming from the bottom of the spike with some of the spike in bud, some in flower and some going to seed. **Ht.:** 18 inches to 5 feet. **Lvs.:** Long, narrow, gray-green, growing up many branches. **Areas:** IV,VIII. Very common along the San Andreas fault line from Leona Valley to Big Rock Creek. Leaves were cooked by indians and eaten after many water rinses; otherwise it caused vomiting.
Date_____Location_____

Slender Keel Fruit
Tropidocarpum gracile

Fls.: Tiny 4-petaled, yellow flower, barely 1/4 inch in diameter. **Ht.:** 1 to 3 inches. **Lvs.:** Deeply notched. **Areas:** I, VIII, X, XI, XII, XIII, XIV. Produces a slender seedpod with a slight curve, 1 to 2 inches long. Found in open fields on the west side of the Antelope Valley and off of Bacchus Road in among other small plants such as Filaree and Pygmy-Leaved Lupine.
Date_____Location_____

Jewel Flower
Caulanthus coulteri
Fls.: 4 little-noticed, winglike petals come out of a small green tube hanging from a thin stalk; the dark purple cluster of buds at the tip of the stalk provides the beauty of this plant. **Ht.:** 12 to 30 inches. **Lvs.:** Notched, spear-shaped with the broad part of the leaf almost enveloping the stalk; many branches from base. **Areas:** XII,X. Grows with Phacelia, Coreopsis and Poppies in the early part of the season.
Date_____Location_____

Desert Candle
(Squaw Cabbage)
Caulanthus inflatus

Fls.: Petals are insignificant on dark red pods on the sides of a thick, yellow, hollow stalk; the dark red buds at the top of the stalk are the "flame" of the candle. **Ht.**: Up to 3 feet. **Lvs.**: Large, spear-shaped on the bottom third of the plant, several branches from near the base of the plant. **Areas:** III. When the rains are good, these plants may grow thickly over many acres. Otherwise, they will be very scattered. The pioneers, reportedly, cooked the leaves like mustard greens, making a very strong-tasting dish.
Date_____Location_____

Rock Cress
Arabis pulchra

Fls.: Several rose-colored, tube-shaped flowers open near the top of a crooked stalk; buds form the tip of the stalk. **Ht.**: Up to 2 feet. **Lvs.**: Gray-green, narrow, pointed, larger at base than up the stalk. **Areas:** scattered throughout IV,VIII,X & XIII.
Date_____Location_____

Spectacle Pod
Dithyrea californica

Fls.: Typical white mustard flower growing in racemes at the ends of spreading, weak stems. **Ht.**: 4 to 12 inches. **Lvs.**: Deeply notched, mostly basal. **Areas:** II,III. Easily identified by spectacle-shaped seedpod. Grows in sandy areas in among the Sand Verbena.
Date_____Location_____

Fringe Pod
(Lace Pod)
Thysanocarpus curvipes

Fls.: Minute, white turning to purple in dangling racemes. **Ht.**: 8 to 20 inches. **Lvs.**: Basal leaves are long and narrow with rough edges; upper leaves clasp the stem. **Areas:** Widespread. Again, the best identification point is the rounded, fringed seedpod.
Date_____Location_____

Shepherds Purse (alien)
Capsella bursa-pastoris

Fls.: Very tiny mustard flowers at the ends of exceptionally weak stems. **Ht.:** 4 to 14 inches. **Lvs.:** Long, with rough edges, mostly basal. **Areas:** Amost all areas, including being a weed in city lawns. Easily identified by the triangular seedpods which resemble an inverted shepherd's purse. Native of Europe.

Date_____Location_____

Hoary Cress (alien)
(Whitetop, White Weed, Perennial Peppergrass)
Cardaria draba

Fls.: White mustard flowers in racemes. The stems of the lower flowers are longer than the upper ones so the flowers are all on the same level. **Ht.:** 8 to 20 inches. **Lvs.:** 1 1/2 to 3 inches long, rough edges. The entire plant has a grayish-green, soft, hairy appearance. **Areas:** VII,IX. Grows in large masses in very wet areas. Native of Central Europe and Asia. Spreads from roots and seeds and causes serious problems as a weed in many areas of the United States.

Date_____Location_____

Water Cress (alien)
Rorippa nasturtium-aquaticum

Fls.: Small, white, in flattened racemes. **Ht.:** 4 to 12 inches, spreading. **Lvs.:** Shiny, opposite, 1 1/2 to 5 inches long. **Areas:** Grows in water or on muddy banks of many quiet stream coming out of the mountains. Used in salads to give a peppery taste. The botanical name nasturtium comes from the Latin nasi tortium meaning "distortion of the

nose"–a reference to its pungency. Not related to the garden Nasturtium although its leaves may also give a sharp taste to salads.

Date_____Location_____

Shield Cress   (alien)
Lepidium perfoliatum

Fls.: Typical mustard growth with 4-petaled, yellow flowers at ends of branches; seedpods are below the flowers. **Ht.:** 6 inches to 2 feet. **Lvs.:** Basal leaves are finely cut, simple pinnate; upper leaves are round and clasp the stalk. **Areas:** VI. Turns reddish at maturity and is sometimes confused with Punctured Bract.

Date_____Location_____

Desert Alyssum
Lepidium fremontii

Fls.: White, fragrant petals less than 1/4 inch long, densely covering a many-branched, green-stemmed, rounded bush; seedpods are typical of mustard family. Flower somewhat resembles the domestic Sweet Alyssum, but it is not related. **Ht.:** 8 to 20 inches. **Lvs.:** 1 to 2 inches long, very narrow. **Areas:** I,III,IV. Another of the many plants named after Capt. John C. Fremont, whose botanist discovered it during Fremont's travels through California in the 1840s.

Date_____Location_____

B. CAPER FAMILY (Capparaceae)
Similar to Mustard family but with differently shaped leaves (hand-shaped, with fingers spreading out). Has skunklike smell when mashed. Flowers are irregularly shaped. An inflated seedpod often appears on a stalk in the center of the flower.

Bladder Pod
Isomeris arborea

Fls.: Showy, yellow, in dense clusters at ends of branches, 4 oblong petals, 3/8 to 5/8 inch long, 4 sepals, 6 stamens; blooms from early spring to frost, but most heavily in the spring; inflated, dangling, 1 to 2 inch seedpods are on the plant at the same time as it is flowering; odor offensive to some. **Ht.:** 2 to 8 feet. **Lvs.:** elliptical, gray-green, in 3's on end of stems. **Areas:** VII,IX,X,XII,XV. Because of its showy blossoms, its long blooming period, its dense foliage and its tolerance to drought,this is an excellent native plant for any garden.

Date_____Location_____

C. FOUR O'CLOCK FAMILY (Nyctaginaceae)

Funnel-like or tubular flowers with 4 or 5-lobed petals. They are herbs. Leaves grow opposite one another.

Sand Verbena
Abronia villosa

Fls.: 20 or more rose colored, tubular flowers with white centers in an umbel. **Ht.:** 10 to 16 inches, bush may be up to 4 feet across. **Lvs.:** thick, rough, oval, dark green. **Areas:** II,III. Some years, these showy plants may cover large areas of sand in and around Saddleback Buttes State Park and other years may not be seen at all. Two other species, A. micrantha and A. pogonantha which are much lighter in color, may at times be found in the same area. The A. villosa is the same flower that covers large areas in and around Palm Springs and the Anza Borego Desert.

Date_____Location_____

Giant 4 O'Clock
Mirabilis froebelii

Fls.: Many large, showy, magenta or white funnel-like flowers with long stamens tipped with yellow anthers. **Lvs.:** Sticky, heart-shaped, dark green leaves, 1 1/4 to 3 inches long on purple, hairy stems. **Ht.:** Compact bush up to 18 inches and up to 3 feet across. **Areas:** VIII,XI,I,XIII. Flower description above is how us common flower-watchers see the flower. A botanist (Barbara J. Collins in Key to Wildflowers of the Deserts of Southern California, p. 55) describes it much differently: "Several flowers occur inside a large, cuplike involucre that resembles a calyx. Involucres, 1 to 1 1/2 inches long. Flowers, without petals; the calyx is colored and resembles a corolla." Flowers open early evening, bloom all night and close up by about 10:00 A.M. When the flowers open and close actually depends upon temperature and moisture. Pollinated by night-flying moths. The botanical name mirabilis is a Latin word meaning wonderful or marvellous and so they are. Bushes with white flowers are less common but are usually found in the same areas. This species is named after Julius Froebel (1805-1893), nephew of the founder of the kindergarten. He was a German immigrant who was an active member of the California Academy of Sciences.

Date_____Location_____

Wishbone Bush
Mirabilis bigelovii

Fls.: Many peach to light magenta and white funnel-shaped flowers with white throats and long stamens. **Ht.:** Loosely formed bush, 6 to 12 inches high and maybe 18 inches across. **Lvs.:** Oval, opposite, small. **Areas:** IV,VIII,XIV. Common name comes from the wishbone appearance of the stems when they branch. Used by some Shoshone Indian Tribes as a medication for sores and boils. As recorded by Edith Van Allen Murphey in Indian Uses of Native Plants, instructions were to "dry root in sun, grind fine. Peel scab, blow powder on" (p. 44). Was also known as "Impetigo plant."

Date_____Location_____

D. BEDSTRAW OR MADDER FAMILY (Rubiaceae)
Four tiny petals in a tiny cross. Four stamens which are alternate with the petals. Rough, prickly, square stems.

Bedstraw
Galium stellatum

Fls.: Greenish-yellow, 4 petals in a cross, 1/10 inch across, 4 stamens alternate with the petals, rough, prickly, square stems. **Ht.:** 8 to 28 inches. **Lvs.:** Lance-like, less than 3/8 inch long, in a cluster of 4s at joints of stems. **Areas:** VIII. The flowers, leaves and stems are so small that the shrub has almost a lacy appearance. The common name, Bed-straw, is an old English name for all of this genus because they were some-times used instead of straw as bed tick-ing or mattress stuffing.

Date_____Location_____

E. EVENING PRIMROSE FAMILY (Onagraceae)

Four separate petals with 8 stamens. The stigma which is on the end of a long thin style is either a four branched cross or bulblike. Ovary is located well below where the sepals and petals become fused.

Spencer Primrose
Camissonia ignota

Fls.: Bright yellow, 4 individual petals, stamens uneven in length. **Ht.:** Up to 10 inches. **Lvs.:** Thin, narrow, curving. **Areas:** Most. It branches from near the base. The papery bark will split and peel off with age. There are a number of camissonias in the area. They may differ considerably in height and foliage, but do have a similar flower structure. One of these, C. gistorta, grows in Pine Canyon and has a basal rosette of elliptical leaves. Similar features of these plants are the tiny green buds, the yellow, 4-petaled flowers and the red, budlike roll of petals as they mature.

Date_____Location_____

Desert Suncups

Camissonia palmeri

Fls.: Similar to but smaller than the Spencer Primrose. **Ht.:** 1 to 3 inches, but as the plant gets older, the branches may be up to 10 inches long. **Lvs.:** Long, gray-green, broad and wavy. **Areas:** VI,X. Seedpods are surprisingly large compared to the size of the flower.

Date_____Location_____ ___

Mustard-Like Primrose

Camissonia californica

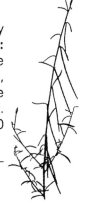

Fls.: 4 small, individual yellow petals on moderately long stems from the stalk. **Ht.:** 2 to 5 feet. **Lvs.:** Mostly on the bottom quarter of the plant. They are long, narrow, and notched. Those above are short, and narrow but not notched. **Areas:** VIII. As the name implies, the plant does resemble a mustard plant. Flowers open in the evening and close before 10:00 A.M. and are very hard to find after that time.

Date_____Location_____

Large Yellow Desert Primrose
Oenothera primiveris

Fls.: Large, showy, lemon yellow, 4-petaled flowers turning orange-red with age; blossoms open in early evening, are open all night and begin closing up the morning of the next day. One anther is in the form of a cross. **Ht.:** 4 to 6 inches. **Lvs.:** Very long, velvety, gray-green, heavily notched with a light colored spine running through the middle of the leaf. Most leaves lie on the ground. **Areas:** II,III. Grows on sandy soil. The species name primiveris describes its early blooming habits.

Date_____Location_____

Hooker Primrose
Oenothera hookeri

Fls.: Golden, 4-petaled flower similar to Large Yellow Desert Primrose, but with flowers formed near the top of strong stalks. **Ht.:** Up to 4 or 5 feet. **Lvs.:** Many narrow, green, pointed leaves with slight saw-toothed edges around the stalk. **Areas:** IV,IX. When these flowers open in early evening, they actually make a slight popping sound. Grow in very moist areas, sometimes with their feet in the water.

Date_____Location_____

Wine Cups
Clarkia purpurea

Fls.: Tiny, deep red or maroon, 4-petaled flowers growing near the top of a thin, erect stalk with few branches. **Ht.:** 6 to 20 inches. **Lvs.:** 1 to 2 inches long, narrow, lying close to the stalk. **Areas:** IX. Grow in small groups not close together. Occasionally, lighter, two-toned red flowers are found. This flower may be confused with Red Maids, which is lighter in color and has 5 petals.

Date_____Location_____

103

Red Ribbons
(Elegant Clarkia)
Clarkia unguiculata
Fls.: 4 reddish-purple, somewhat diamond-shaped petals on stems from a center pod where the 8 stamens are located, buds hanging, flowers erect; numerous flowers surround each stalk two thirds of the way up the stalk; few or no branches. **Ht.:** 12 to 40 inches. **Lvs.:** narrow, veined, alternate. **Areas:** IX. The common name is understandable once you see the flower.
Date_____Location_____

Farewell-to-Spring
(Speckled Clarkia)
Clarkia cylindrica
Fls.: Delicate, bowl-shaped flower with pink on the outer petals fading to white in the center. On some the white is speckled with pink dots. Flowers erect, buds drooping. **Ht.:** 8 to 20 inches. **Lvs.:** Very narrow, 1 to 2 inches long; erect, red stalk with few branches. **Areas:** IX,XV. Sometimes these will blanket whole hillsides. Although this one is not the last flower to bloom in spring (the Giant Four O'Clock might qualify for that honor), it and the Red Ribbons do bloom late in the season.
Date_____Location_____

Dune Primrose
(Birdcage Evening Primrose, Desert Primrose, Devil's Lantern, Lion in a Cage)
Oenothera deltoides
Fls.: Pink buds open in the evening into large, showy white flowers up to 3 inches in diameter. Fragrant, with 4 heart-shaped petals. Bloom until late morning the next day. 8 stamens plus an apparent stamen with a cross at the upper end. **Ht.:** 4 to 12 inches; pale branches spreading up to 40 inches; in season almost completely covered with flowers. **Lvs.:** Gray-green, lancelike, may or may not be toothed. **Areas:** II and VI. Also on rare occasions, west of Sierra Highway near the Lockheed plant. Many times grows with the Sand Verbena in sandy soil. When the plant dries, the branches

curve upward forming a cage-like structure. This is an annual. The seeds are spread by the wind blowing these skeletons across the sands.
Date_____Location_____

California Primrose
Oenothera californica
Fls.: Very similar to the Dune Primrose above, except that the flowers are much more prone to turn pinkish with age. **Ht.:** 4 to 8 inches. **Lvs.:** Gray-green (one subspecies has dark green leaves), long, narrow, may or may not be notched. **Areas:** VIII,X,XI,XII,XIII,XIV. Generally these Primroses are found on the west side of the Valley while the Dune Primrose is found on the east side. These plants are perennial, develop from underground roots and do not form a "birdcage."
Date_____Location_____

Woody Bottlewasher
(Bottle Cleaner)
Camissonia boothii
Fls.:   Many small, white, 4-petaled flowers, on the end of the stalk, turning pink with age. Stamens are not significant; pink buds drooping. Flower cluster begins on short stalk and remains on the end of the stalk as it grows. As petals fall off, a rigid stem together with rigid, horned seedpods are left, making the dried stalk resemble a bottlewasher. **Ht.:** 6 to 14 inches; many stalks, which grow from base. **Lvs.:** Green with whitish cast, 2 to 3 inches long, narrow, mostly on top side of the white stalk; **Areas:** VIII,IX.
Date_____Location_____

Brown-Eyed Primrose
Camissonia claviformis
Fls.: A cluster of small, 4-petaled white flowers, with a small brown spot at the base of the petals; growing on the end of the stalk, buds drooping, stamens prominent. Flower cluster begins on a short stalk and remains on the end of stalk as it grows. As petals fall off, stem becomes a seedpod. Stalk does not form a skeleton as does the Bottlewasher. **Ht.:** 6 to 12 inches, few stalks from base. **Lvs.:** shiny, dark green, broad, 1 to 2 inches long, mostly on bottom third of plant, stalk and stems reddish green. **Areas:** II,VIII,XII. A very common plant which is little noticed. Blooms early in season.
Date_____Location_____

VII. 5 SEPARATE PETALS IN AN IRREGULAR ARRANGEMENT

A. PEA FAMILY (Leguminosae)

The typical pea flower is made up of a large, broad upper petal, which is the banner. The two side petals below the banner are the wings, and the two lower petals join to form a canoelike keel which is called the keel. Leaves are alternate and mostly compound. This large family of plants adds nitrogen to the soil.

Hairy Lotus
Lotus tomentellus

Fls.: Tiny, yellow, with the banner and the keel, barely 3/8 inch diameter, turning to red as they age. **Ht.:** 2 to 3 inches but branches may be 8 to 12 inches long, mostly on the ground. **Lvs.:** Shiny, pinnately compound. **Areas:** I,IIV,VIII,X,XI,XII,XIV. Plants grow among the coreopsis, poppies, and chia and are barely noticeable unless they are massed together. Then they will look like a bright yellow carpet.
Date_____Location_____

Broom Deer Weed
Lotus scoparius ssp.brevialatus

Fls.: Tiny, yellow pea flowers, turning to red, mixed with leaves around reedy branches. **Ht.:** Bushy, up to 3 feet. **Lvs.:** Tiny leaflets with 3, 4 or 5 leaves. **Areas:** IV,VIII,IX,X,XIV. There are many plants commonly called Deer Weed. This particular one grows in the foothills in mid to late season and is bushier than most.
Date_____Location_____

Loco Weed
(Rattleweed)
Astragalus pachypus

Fls.: Tiny, pale yellow flowers with banner and keel clustered around a stem. **Ht.:** Bushy, 12 to 24 inches. **Lvs.:** Long, pinnately compound leaves. **Areas:** X,XI,XII. Common in among California Poppies. Noted for their large yellow seedpods in clusters which seem to invite kids to jump on them to hear them pop.
Date_____Location_____

Desert Rattleweed
(Loco Weed)
Astragalus

There are a number of species of red, purple and pink Astragalus over the entire area which botanists identify by the color and shape of the flower, the color and shape of the seedpod and the color and shape of the leaves. I have limited myself to describing features which are common to all. **Fls.:** Pea flower with the banner and the keel on a raceme. **Ht.:** 6 to 18 inches, usually many-branched, spreading. **Lvs.:** opposite on a stem called "odd-pinnate;" seedpod usually inflated and hollow,but may be long like a peapod. **Areas:** All. The common name comes from the seeds rattling in the seedpod. Loco Weed means mad or crazy weed in Spanish and comes from the behavior of cattle and horses after having eaten some of these plants. Fortunately, most animals pass this plant by unless there is a serious shortage of other forage. But once tasted, it seems to become addictive. Symptons are a disheveled coat, poor eyesight, staggering and sometimes, especially with horses, uncontrolable fits of temper.

Date_____Location_____

Pin-Point Clover
Trifolium gracilentum

Fls.: Pink to reddish-purple, pealike flowers in a tight cluster making up a head which is 1/4 to 3/8 inch long at the end of a naked stem. The head is a little like a strawberry with the bottom of the head a wooly green. **Ht.:** 4 to 16 inches. **Lvs.:** 3, oval, in a cluster called palmately 3-foliolate, growing part way up the stem. **Areas:** VII,VIII,X,XIV. Usually found in small groups in among other flowers.

Date_____Location_____

Birdsfoot Trefoil (alien)
(Birdsfoot Lotus)
Lotus corniculatus

Fls.: Pea flower with enlarged keel, some yellow, some red with red predominating, in clusters on long stems. **Ht.:** 6 to 8 inches, runners up to 2 feet. **Lvs.:** 3 oblong leaflets per leaf. **Areas:** IX,X. Road-side plant forming showy mat of flowers.

Date_____Location_____

Lupine
Lupinus

The botanical name is from the Latin word lupus meaning wolf or robber because the early Romans first observed lupine growing on barren soil and concluded that the plant robbed the soil of nutrients. Later it was found that, as a legume, it added nutrients to the soil and has been used as a soil conditioner ever since. There are 48 species of lupine listed by Dr. Philip Munz in A Flora of Southern California. There are another 30 or 40 species statewide. They all have alternate, palmately compound leaves and flowers with a banner and a keel in a raceme. In the Antelope Valley we probably have at least a dozen varieties. Some lupine are difficult to identify as they differ only by the size and shape of the seed or the configuration of the flowers in the raceme. These may only be identified with the aid of a microscope. Because of this, most flower-watchers lacking the tools of a botanist, have to be content with knowing that the flower is a lupine and not concern themselves with the species. Listed below are the most common and easily identifiable lupine in the Antelope Valley.

Royal Desert Lupine
Lupinus odoratus

Fls.: Blue to purple with yellow spot on banner. **Ht.:** 6 to 12 inches. **Lvs.:** On long stems from base. **Areas:** II,III,VI. An annual plant, growing on the desert floor from Lancaster east to the county line with most common spot now around 180th St. East and Ave M. In past years many vacant blocks of Lancaster were covered with masses of this lupine. The botanical name of the species comes from the fact that the flower is very fragrant.

Date_____Location_____

Elegant Lupine
Lupinus concinnus

Fls.: Typical lupine flower with the banner and keel in a raceme, colored lilac and red-purple with a little yellow in the center of the banner. **Ht.:** 2 to 8 inches. **Lvs.:** Typical palmately compound lupine leaves, very hairy; many-branched, hairy stalks. **Areas:** XI,XIV. A great many blue lupine will photograph pink or red but this is one of the few that is really in the red zone.

Date_____Location_____

Pygmy-Leaved Lupine
Lupinus bicolor

Fls.: Raceme is 1/4 to 3 inches long, blue with a white dot in the center of banner. **Ht.:** 4 to 10 inches. **Lvs.:** Small but many on each plant. **Areas:** VIII,X,XII,XIII. On the west side of the Antelope Valley beginning about 90th St. West and going to about 200th St. West, hundreds of acres are sometimes covered with nothing but this plant. The flowers are so small and the leaves so many that all one tends to notice is a blue-green ground cover extending well into the distance. It is worthwhile to stop and examine these beautiful little flowers close up. These, unlike many lupine, will record a true blue on film.

Date_____Location_____

Bentham Lupine
Lupinus benthamii

Fls.: Bright, showy blue with a white topknot, banner has a vertical white stripe through the middle. **Ht.:** 12 to 18 inches. **Lvs.:** Very narrow palmate leaves. **Areas:** XV. Many years this very showy flower covers whole hillsides off of Gorman Post Road. These along with the Coreopsis and California Poppies make this area a flower-watcher's dream. It also photographs a true blue.

Date_____Location_____

Adonis Lupine
(Bush Lupine)
Lupinus excubitus

Fls.: Petals are blue to violet to orchid with a yellow center on the banner, long racames. **Ht.:** 2 to 5 feet. **Lvs.:** Gray-green, on a very woody plant, could be considered a shrub. **Area:** XII,XIII. There are number of other Bush Lupine notably on the hills on the north side of Elizabeth Lake, in Bouquet Canyon and in fields along Highway 138 near the western foothills which I have yet to indentify. One growing in Pine Canyon is *L. albifrons.* Rarely do any of these photograph a true color.

Date_____Location_____

White Lupine
Lupinus horizontalis

Fls.: Typical lupine raceme, white to pale purple. **Ht.** 3 to 8 inches; **Lvs.:** Typical lupine, palmate leaf. **Areas;** IV,VIII,X,XIII. Another lupine *L. pallidus* is whitish to pale blue or yellow.

Date_____Location_____

B. VIOLET FAMILY (Violaceae)

All members of this family which includes domestic violets had two upper petals, two lateral petals, and a single lower lip petal. Only one species is listed as native to the Antelope Valley.

Johnny Jump-up
Viola pendunculata

Fls.: Small, orange-yellow flowers look like the domestic violet. **Ht.:** 4 to 10 inches. **Lvs.:** Spade-shaped on a long stem. **Area:** IX. Perennial plant grows from a rhizome. It is reported that the Indians ate the leaves as greens.

Date_____Location_____

VIII. 5 SEPARATE PETALS IN A REGULAR ARRANGEMENT

A. PURSLANE FAMILY (Portulacaceae)

Two sepals; five to many petals; five to many stamens. Plant tends to be succulent. Stems sometimes pass through the center of round, fleshy leaves.

Red Maids   (alien)
Calandrinia ciliata

Fls.: Rose red and round-tipped petals, many stamens, 2 sepals. **Ht.:** Spreading, up to 16 inches. **Lvs.:** Alternate, narrow, lancelike with a point. **Areas:** I,VIII,X,XI,XIII,XIV. Rarely found in groups; mostly scattered among other flowers; grows throughout the season.

Date_____Location_____

Miner's Lettuce
Claytonia perfoliata

Fls.: Tiny cluster of white buds and flowers projecting through a rounded leaf. **Ht.:** 2 to 12 inches. **Lvs.:** Top leaves are shiny, dark-green, sometimes succulent; basal leaves, short and narrow. **Areas:** VIII, IX,X,XII. On north slopes in moist areas. Early miners ate it as a salad or cooked it to supplement diet of bacon and beans.

Date_____Location_____

B. MALLOW FAMILY (Malvaceae)

Hollyhocklike flowers, maplelike leaves (veins originating from a central point), characterize this family. Stamens are fused into a tube that surrounds the pistil. The fruit splits into several pie-shaped wedges at maturity.

Apricot Mallow
(Desert Hollyhock, Desert Mallow, Desert Globemallow)
Sphaeralcea ambiqua

Fls.: Many apricot to deep apricot to orange or sometimes deep red, bowl shaped (1/2 to 1 1/2 inches in diameter) on erect but leaning stalks, mixed with buds and leaves. **Ht.:** 15 to 30 inches. **Lvs.:** Small, dark green, maplelike. **Areas:** II,III in small to large groups, mid to late season. Many grew in east Palmdale,which is now covered with housing tracts. Occasionally, a flower-watcher will observe a large shrub with the same leaves and flowers as the Apricot Mallow in among these flowers. This shrub is apparently a subspecies of the one listed.
Date_____Location_____

Bush Mallow
Malacothamnus densiflorus

Fls.: 5 rose pink petals in dense clusters, up a spike, many buds with few flowers open. **Ht.:** 3 to 6 feet with many branches. **Lvs.:** Gray, maplelike, many times with one leaf growing out of the flower cluster; **Areas:** IV,V,VIII.
Date_____Location_____

Checker Bloom
Sidalcea neomexicana

Fls.: Pink, noticeably veined, bowl-shaped flowers growing closely togather usually on the topside of a horizontal branch. **Ht.:** 30 inches with branches as long as 4 feet. **Lvs.:** Two kinds: some five-fingered and deeply lobed, others five- fingered without lobes. **Areas:** IX,XII. Another species can be found in Leona Valley that is much shorter and has petals which are more ragged.
Date_____Location_____

C. GERANIUM FAMILY (Geraniaceae)
Flower parts in a pattern of fives. (5 petals; 5, 10 or 15 stamens; 5 seeds).
Seeds have long tails which coil at maturity.

Red Stem Filaree (alien)
(Heronsbill, Clocks, Scissors, Alfilaria, Alfilerilla,
Pin Clover, Storksbill, Pin Grass)
Erodium cicurarium

Fls.: Pink or magenta, about 1/2 inch in diameter, 5 separate petals, flowers in clusters. **Ht.:** 2 to 10 inches, spreading. **Lvs.:** Fernlike, hairy on underside. **Areas:** Almost all. One of the first introduced plants; from the Mediterranean Area; an excellent forage plant. The common names and the botanical name refer to or describe the 1 1/2 inch seedpod which, while green, is like a pin or a bill but which, when dry breaks down into 5 seeds with curled tails that easily attaches to the fur of animals. When wet, these tails uncurl like a hand of a clock. It is so efficient in reseeding itself that, within 50 years of introduction, it had spread over most of California below 4,000 feet elevation. Of an early morning in spring, these tiny flowers are so thick that they form a magenta carpet if the ground has not been cultivated for some time. On loose soil, the leaves are much more prominent and tend to hide the flowers.
Date_____Location_____

D. CALTROP FAMILY (Zygophyllaceae)
Flowers on plan of 5's with 10 stamens. Leaves are pinnate—a group of leaves growing opposite each other on a stem.

Creosote Bush
Larrea tridentata

Fls.: Yellow, 5 individual petals, mostly cupped, about 1/4 inch long, 5 sepals, 10 stamens; white, furry seedpods form while flowers are still on the shrub. **Ht.:** 2 to 9 feet. **Lvs.:** Green, shiny, strongly scented, opposite, 3/8 inch long or less growing on gray, brittle limbs with corky rings at nodes. **Areas:** Widespread over Desert floor. Depending upon how one looks at it, some of these may be the oldest living plants in the world. Large circles of these shrubs are found throughout the desert. Ones

found near California City are estimated to have started with a single plant 11,000 years ago with the present ones being clones from the original plant. There is some validity to this claim, when you consider that the previous "oldest living thing" was the 4,800 year old Bristlecone Pine in the White Mountains near Bishop, California. It is not the living part of the tree that is 4,800 years old, but rather a part of the tree that died many years ago.
Date_____Location_____

E. BUTTERCUP FAMILY (Ranunculaceae)
This family has exceedingly variable characteristics that can only be described in botanical terms. Of the plants listed here, there is considerable difference between the larkspurs and the clematis.

Scarlet Larkspur
Delphinium cardinale
Fls.: Bright, showy, scarlet, 5-lobed flower with the back end shaped like a spur or (to the Greeks) a dolphin. Many flowers surround a naked stalk. The stem attaches between the tail or spur and the open end of the flower. **Ht.:** 3 to more than 6 feet. **Lvs.:** Basal, withered when blooming. **Areas:** IX. Much more common in the canyons leading into the San Fernando Valley, but spectacular when found blooming in Bouquet Canyon. Blooms in late season.
Date_____Location_____

Parish Larkspur
(Parish's Desert Delphinium)
Delphinium parishii
Fls.: Behind pale blue petals is a spur; the stem attaches to the flower between the petals and spur; many flowers in raceme. **Ht.:** 18 to 24 inches. **Lvs.:** Large, 3 to 5 oblong lobes, mostly basal, few left when flower blooms. **Areas:** IV and near the Palmdale reservoir. The Scandinavians and the English named this flower after the spur of the lark, whereas the Spanish know it as *espuela del caballero* or "the horseman's spur." The botanical name came from the Greeks, who called it the dolphin flower. The Greeks had a legend about a fisherman who saved a dolphin's life. Later when the fisherman died, the dolphin took the body to King Neptune. Out of the grave grew these flowers.
Date_____Location_____

Clematis
(Virgin's Bower, Pipe Stem Clematis)
Clematis lasiantha

Fls.: No petals, 4 petal-like sepals, many long stamens, both sepals and stamens are creamy yellow on long, slightly hairy stems; seeds have long tails which make a ball about 2 inches in diameter. **Ht.:** Vines have many branches and may be up to 15 feet long. **Lvs.:** Variable, 3 to 5 leaflets in a grouping, green, shiny, notched or lobed. **Areas:** IV,V,IX. Usually seen growing up over and crowning scrub oak. A very showy, beautiful plant both in flower and in seed.

Date_____Location_____

F. SUMAC FAMILY (Anacardiaceae)
This family consists of shrubs and small trees. Although insignificant, the flowers are in a pattern of 5's with 5 petals, 5 sepals and 5 stamens.

Squaw Bush
Rhus trilobata

Fls.: Pale yellow, in clusters at ends of branches, 1/2 to 1 inch long, appearing before the leaves; fruit is reddish and very small. **Ht.:** 3 to 5 feet, up to 8 feet across. **Lvs.:** Deciduous, 3 or 5 leaves on a single stem from a branch with smooth brown bark, up to 3 inches long, strong odor when crushed. **Areas:** Common in canyons in foothills below 3,500 feet elevation. Can easily be confused with Poison Oak (see next page). Branches are drooping and sometimes may root from the tips when covered with dirt. Indians used the branches in basket weaving (they pruned the plant to promote straight stalks), and a pink lemonadelike drink was made from the fruit. Twigs rolled in their leaves and boiled with pine pitch made the best black dye.

Date_____Location_____

Poison Oak
Toxicodendron disversilobum

Fls.: Greenish-white, drooping bunches of flowers, each flower having a separate stem, appear with the leaves. **Ht.:** 2 to 6 feet. **Lvs.:** Shiny, notched, in a pattern of three's with the lower two leaves being smaller than the upper one. **Areas:** Can be found in most canyons in the mountains. Most prominent growth is probably in Bouquet Canyon where it is found in thick stands on both sides of the stream below the dam. Leaves turn bright red and yellow as early as September. Anyone who hikes in the hill country is advised to learn to identify this shrub and stay clear of it because contact causes a severe dermatitis in most people at any time of the year. One theory is that more than one contact is necessary to develop a rash. Smoke from the burning plants is especially dangerous. **Just remember: Leaves of three, let it be.** Indians used the plant medicinally and some reportedly were immune to it. They marked their faces with poison oak juice before tattooing.

Date_____Location_____

G. STONECROP FAMILY (Crassulaceae)
Leaves and stems are succulent. Four or five petals and sepals with as many, or twice as many stamens as petals.

Live Forever
Dudlelya cymosa ssp. minor

Fls.: 20 to 35 small, pointed, yellow-orange flowers make up a flower head of about 3 inches across that grows from a single succulent stem, several stems per plant start from underneath the rosette of leaves. **Ht.:** 6 to 8 inches. **Lvs.:** A rosette of light green or brownish succulent leaves at the base with tiny leaves up the stem. **Areas:** V,XII. Found on banks and in rocky foothill areas. At least two other species may be found in the area. One with deep red flowers may be found along Angeles Forest Highway and the other is a very large plant with bluish-gray leaves and stalk is in Bouquet Canyon.

Date_____Location_____

H. PINK FAMILY (Caryophyllaceae)
The 4 or 5 petals are often notched or deeply divided. Five to ten stamens. Annual or perennial herbs with swollen nodes. Leaves are opposite.

115

Indian Pinks
Silene laciniata

Fls.: Showy, scarlet petals, deeply cleft **Ht.:** 6 to 8 inches, spreading, weak stems. **Lvs.:** Narrow, linear, opposite. **Area:** IX. Perennial, grows from a fleshy taproot. Similar to garden pinks.
Date_____Location_____

I. ROSE FAMILY (Rosaceae)
5 petals and 5 sepals with many stamens make up the regularly shaped flowers. Leaves are alternate, often compound.

California Wild Rose
Rosa californica

Fls. Pink or rose-colored, simple 5-petaled, 3/4 to 1 inch long petals, many stamens. **Ht.:** 3 to 9 feet, usually in a thorny thicket. **Lvs.:** Typical rose leaf: green, shiny, with serrated edges, 5 or 7 leaflets form a com-compound leaf with 4 or 6 opposite and 1 at the top end. Grow on thorny branches. **Areas:** Moist can- yons in the foothills and mountains up to 6,000 feet. Most likely spots are Bouquet Canyon and Big Rock Creek. Identification of this plant is simple because of its similarity to the domestic rose. Spanish priests called them Rosas de Castilla as they are similar to wild roses in Spain. Spaniards and Indians ate the rose hips (seedpods) or macuatas, as they called them, raw or after a little bit of cooking. Adelbert von Chamisso, who named the California Poppy, also gave the botanical name to this plant.
Date_____Location_____

Cliffrose
Cowania mexicana

Fls.: 5 distinct, cream to sulfur yellow petals; numerous orange stamens; flowers less than 3/4 inch across, almost covering the branches from bottom to top. **Ht.:** A woody shrub, 1 to 9 feet. **Lvs.:** Up to 1/2 inch long, deeply divided or lobed, green on top, gray underneath. **Areas:** IV. This is an important browse plant for cattle and deer.
Date_____Location_____

Chamise
(Greasewood)
Adenostoma fasciculatum

Fls.: White to cream, turning rust colored as seeds mature, in compact 1 1/2 to 4 inch long clusters, on ends of branches. **Ht.:** Woody shrub, 2 to 12 feet. **Lvs.:** Sharply pointed, not much over 1/4 inch long in numerous clusters along almost the entire lenth of each branch. **Areas:** One of the most common shrubs in any chaparral growth below 5,000 feet elevation. It is highly flammable, causing real problems for brushfire fighters. After fires, the plant usually grows back from the roots, some- times forming thickets almost impenetrable to man or large animals.

Date_____Location_____

J. LOASA FAMILY (Loasaceae)
5 to 10 Petals with 5 sepals and many stamens. The irregularly shaped leaves are covered with short, barbed hairs.

Comet Blazing Star
(Whitestem Mentzelia)
Mentzelia albicaulis

Fls.: Small yellow-orange petals with an orange throat, maybe 5/8 inch across. **Ht.:** Erect, 6 to 18 inches. **Lvs.:** Notched, pointed, few per branch. **Areas:** Almost all. There are a number of species of Blazing Star in the Valley, all of which are very similar in appearance. Other species found here are the Venus Blazing Star (M. nitens), Yellow Comet (M. affinis) and Apollo Blazing Star (M. albicaulis ssp. heliophila). Because of the similarities of these flowers Dr. Bob Gustafson, botanist for the Los Angeles Natural History Museum comments that they are difficult to identify and that, to give them their proper botanical name, "It is important to collect mature plants with seed capsules already formed."

Date_____Location_____

Giant Blazing Star.
Mentzelia laevicaulis

Fls.: Large, bright, shiny, lemon yellow, symmetrical, 5-petaled flowers in clusters of 2 or 3 at the end of stiff branches, many stamens, 5 of the outer stamens resemble narrow petals. **Ht.**: 2 to 3 1/2 feet. **Lvs.**: Lanceshaped, toothed, 3 to 7 inches long, covered with barbed hairs growing from a much branched plant with shiny, almost white stems. **Areas:** Most prominent location is Big Rock Creek in late spring and throughout the summer. This rather unattractive plant produces a beautiful flower that opens in the evening and closes before 10:00 A.M.

Date_____Location_____

K. CARROT FAMILY (Apiaceae, formerly Umbelliferae)
Umbrellalike clusters of many small 5-petaled flowers called umbels. 5 stamens. Has either 5 sepals or none. These aromatic herbs commonly have hollow stems. There are a number of these plants throughout the Antelope Valley that are very similar to the one listed below.

Wild Parsley
Lomatium mohavense

Fls.: Tiny yellow flowers in an umbel form a dense crown, 1 1/2 to 2 inches across. **Ht.**: 4 to 16 inches. **Lvs.**: Green, lacy or fernlike. **Areas:** III,VIII,X,XI,XII, XIV. This plant commonly has yellow flowers, but occasionally may be found with purplish flowers.

Date_____Location_____

IX. 5 UNITED PETALS IN AN IRREGULAR SHAPE

A. MINT FAMILY (Labiatae)
The most significant features are the leaves (arranged opposite each other on square stems) and the mint or sagelike smell when mashed. Many times small 5-petaled flowers grow out of a pod through which grows the stem. Most have 4 stamens, of two different lengths. This very large and popular family includes many domestic plants such as spearment and peppermint, as well as wild plants.

Chia
Salvia columbariae

Fls.: Many tiny blue flowers with white on lower petal grow from a purple pod, as many as 5 pods per stalk. The square stalk grows through the middle of all pods except for the top one. **Ht.:** 6 to 24 inches. **Lvs.:** Opposite, mostly basal, up to 4 inches long with the stems as long as the leaves. **Areas:** IV,V,VII,X,XI,XII,XIV. Grows in great fields after a fire. Seen in smaller groups, usually in disturbed soil, in areas which have not recently burned. Seeds of this plant and a related species, *S. mexicana*, were an important food to the Indians and early settlers. They are very nutritious and are easily digested. Some Indian tribes believed that a tablespoon of chia seed would give a warrior enough energy to go on a 24-hour forced march. Cakes of ground Chia seed were thought to be suitable gifts to the gods as well as very important people. Cortez was given cakes of Chia when he first landed in Mexico. When moistened, seeds become mucilaginous and were placed under the eyelid just before retiring to clean out the dirt in the eyes. Poultices of Chia seed were made to draw out the poison from a gunshot wound. A popular drink in Mexico called Agua de Chia is made with water, Chia seed, a little lemon, a little sugar and a sprinkling of powdered cinnamon. Chia seed can be bought at health food stores today.

Date_____Location_____

Thistle Sage
(Persian Prince)
Salvia carduacea

Fls.: Many blue flowers grow out of a large, white, wooly pod, long stamens with orange anthers, as many as 6 pods per stalk (usually 2 or 3), with the square stem going through each pod but the top one. **Ht.:** 6 to 26 inches. **Lvs.:** Large, wooly, opposite, mostly basal. **Areas:** IV, XIV. In this case the botanical name, literally translated means Thistle Sage. Seeds were used in much the same way as Chia. Usually grows together in good-sized groupings. The name Persian Prince comes from the look of the wooly pods, which reminds some people of a turban.

Date_____Location_____

White Sage
Salvia apiana

Fls.: Delicate, irregularly shaped white to pale blue flowers on upper two thirds of tall stalks are intermixed with leaves; stamens curve out of the blossoms. **Ht.:** 2 to 5 feet. **Lvs.:** Fragrant, gray-green, lancelike, many tall stalks growing from leafy base that can be seen year around. **Areas:** VIII and Big Rock Creek.
Date_____Location_____

Pennyroyal
Monardella exilis

Fls: Tiny tubular-shaped flowers in a cluster, surrounded by large bracts with white and green veins. **Ht.:** 4 to 8 inches. **Lvs.:** Gray-green, opposite, oblong and lancelike. **Areas:** II,XIV. Grows late in the season, many times in large groupings. One of the most fragrant flowers to be found in the area. Jane Pinheiro says, "Desert Pennyroyal has chalk white edges and markings on the calyx petals which surround the composite head of small lacy white blossoms that open from the outer edge of the head first, thus giving the effect of a tiny old fashioned bouquet with its white lace frame.... [When] brushed or bruised [it gives] off a strong aromatic scent which to some, including me, is pleasant, though to some it is quite offensive." Another species, called Mustang Mint (M. lanceolata), is smaller and not as fragrant.
Date_____Location_____

Horehound (alien)
Marrubium vulgare

Fls.: Tiny flowers in several doughnutlike clusters around a square stem, each just above a pair of leaves. **Ht.:** 8 inches to 30 inches. **Lvs.:** Pairs of gray oval leaves with a crinkly surface, many stalks grow from a leafy base. **Areas:** VIII,IX,X. Used to make old- fashioned Horehound Candy.
Date_____Location_____

Blue Sage
(Desert Sage, Great Basin Blue Sage, Purple Sage)
Salvia dorrii

Fls.: Fragrant, blue, 2-lipped flowers up to 1/2 inch long grow out of purplish pods through which the square stem grows; as many as 6 pods may be on one stem. **Ht.:** Broad shrub 1 to 3 feet high. **Lvs.:** Gray, opposite, fragrant, up to 5/8 inch long growing thickly on woody stalks. **Areas:** IV,V,VIII,XIV. A nice landscape shrub in a dry corner of the yard.

Date_____Location_____

Paper Bag Bush
(Bladder Sage)
Salarzaria mexicana

Fls.: Cream-colored with a purple lip, up to 3/4 inch, in large bunches at ends of branches, along with cream-colored, papery, inflated-looking fruit or seed-pods. **Ht.:** up to 3 1/2 feet. **Lvs.:** Sparse on most of bush, thicker near the flowers, light green, lancelike, opposite, up to 5/8 inch grow on much branched, dry looking shrub. **Areas:** IV,VII,VIII,XIV. This shrub is known equally well by both common names, both of which are appropriate because of the seedpods.

Date_____Location_____

Wooly Blue Curls
Trichostema parishii

Fls.: Numerous long spikes of fragrant, wooly, violet flowers, out of which grow extremely long, curving bluish-purple stamens. **Ht.:** Up to 4 feet. **Lvs.:** Many and narrow, 1 to 3 1/2 inches, resembling the garden herb, rosemary. **Areas:** VII,IX. Flower-watchers may also find a shorter species, T. lanatum, which is a more rounded bush. Either is very appropriate as a landscape shrub. Indians used vapors from boiling the plant in water to clear sinus cavities, to stop nosebleeds and to cure headaches. The Spanish considered it to be a panacea. They used it to make an ointment, a liniment and to cure wounds.

Date_____Location_____

B. FIGWORT OR SNAPDRAGON FAMILY (Scrophulariaceae)

4 or 5 united petals in a 2-lipped corolla (flower tube), 4 stamens, sometimes with a fifth sterile stamen fused to corolla. Many variable features.

Indian Paintbrush
(Desert Paintbrush)
Castilleja chromosa

Fls.: The petals are difficult to locate. The bracts and calyxes give the plant its orange-red color. It looks that a stalk of ragged leaves that has been dipped in orange-red paint with a little yellow coming out on the upper leaves. **Ht.:** 4 to 16 inches. **Lvs.:** Short, narrow, hairy, mostly at the base, some extend up the stalk. **Areas:** IV,V,VIII,IX,X. Blooms for most of the season. Although the leaves and the roots are capable of furnishing all the required nutrition, most of the time it is a parasite, latching onto the roots of nearby shrubs.

Date_____Location_____

Yellow Paintbrush
Castilleja plagiotoma

A somewhat rare plant that, except for its color, is very similar to the Indian Paintbrush (C. chromosa). The flower spike is greenish-yellow and the plant usually grows near or up through shrubs. It also is a partial parasite in that it gets some of its nutrients from the roots of other plants.

Date_____Location_____

Wooly Paintbrush
Castillefa foliolosa

Fls.: Very similar to Indian Paintbrush except the whole plant has a wooly appearance. **Ht.:** 4 to 12 inches. **Lvs.:** Short, narrow, hairy, mostly at the base, some extend up the stalk. **Areas:** X. Easy to spot in the chaparral.

Date_____Location_____

Owl's Clover
Orthocarpus purpurascens ssp. ornatus

Fls.: Compact, maroon-colored bracts cover most of the stalk. The inner parts are deep maroon, and the tips are a lighter maroon. The lower lip of the corolla is white with a beak and two "owl's eyes." **Ht.:** 4 to 8 inches. **Lvs.:** Alternate on lower part of stalk, not too prominent. **Areas:** VIII,X,XII,XIII,XIV. This one is easy to confuse with the Paintbrush, but really it is quite a different flower. Usually grows very close together in large masses. Not a parasite (as is the paintbrush) and not a clover. Probably the Spanish name, Escobitas, meaning little whisk brooms is more appropriate for this flower. Yellow-tipped Owl's Clover grows east of Edward's Air Force Base.

Date_____Location_____

Common Monkey Flower
(Seepspring Monkey Flower)
Mimulus guttatus

Fls.: Showy, bright yellow trumpet flowers with purple or brown dots in the throat. **Ht.:** 1 to 2 feet. **Lvs.:** Large, thick, opposite. **Areas:** Wide- spread in moist areas, notably areas IV, VIII, IX, X, XV. Sometimes one has to use a little imagination, but the name "monkey flower" comes from some people seeing a monkey's face when looking into the flower.

Date_____Location_____

Bush Monkey Flower
(Sticky Monkey Flower)
Mimulus longiflorus

Fls.: Large, showy, 2-lipped, lemon yellow, trumpet flow-ers. **Ht.:** Shrub, 1 to 4 feet. **Lvs.:** Sticky, opposite, lance-like, thick on the branches. **Areas:** IV,IX. Grows in rocky places in canyons. Blooms very heavily for a relatively long period of time in the spring. A related species with orange flowers covers the hills in the Sepulveda Pass.

Date_____Location_____

Fairy Trumpet
Mimulus bigelovii

Fls.: Delicate trumpet flower with lobes for petals. Tip of stigma forms two flaps that often close when touched. **Ht.:** 2 to 10 inches. **Lvs.:** Sparse, small, opposite, on a threadlike stem. **Areas:** II,IV,X. Grows with Parry Gilia and other belly flowers in gravely soil. Jane Pinheiro writes, "Nodding nearby [to the Parry Gilia] one usually finds the inch long magenta trumpet shaped blossoms of the Bigelow Mimulus . . . dancing on one to three inch red brown stems that rise from a rosette of two to six red hairy backed, smooth faced, blue-green leaves. Plants are usually balanced in growth habits, that is, they bear two opposite blossoms, leaves, or branches. Two yellow stripes mark the under throat of the blossom. Agitated in a breeze, these Mimulus remind one of dainty ballet dancers. Very rarely one finds a blond plant with white trumpets cavorting with its ruddy sisters."

Date_____Location_____

Chinese Houses
Collinsia heterophylla

Fls.: Several circles of flowers around a thin stalk, two large light to dark lavender petals below and three small petals (white, lavender or mixed) above. **Ht.:** 4 to 20 inches. **Lvs.:** Opposite, lancelike. **Areas:** VI,IX,X,XII. Jane Pinheiro's description of Chinese Houses is as follows: It is "so called because the blossoms grow in whorls of diminishing size up the stem and 'resemble the architecture of Chinese pagodas'. These tiny denizens of the desert range in size from a single whorl of five to seven blossoms on a plant an inch high to a symmetrically branching plant carrying a central spike of five or six tiers of bloom and around ten inches tall. Its leaves are smooth and bright, dark green, with brown tinged, saw-toothed edges, that curve backward. The blossoms are pert little things, having two petals standing upright, parallel to the stem and a three-in-one petal, curving downward. The throat of the flower is cream or white, and the lower petals and the edges of the upper petals are lavender or pinkish."

Date_____Location_____

Scarlet Bugler
Penstemon centranthifolius
Fls.: Many red, tubelike flowers hanging from a single stalk; 1 to 1 1/2 inches; plant has many stalks. **Ht.:** 12 to 40 inches. **Lvs.:** Opposite, gray-green, clasp stalk with earlike lobes. **Areas:** IV,V,VIII,IX,X,XIV. A similar species, Eaton's Firecracker (P. eatonii) may be found at higher elevations. Eaton's Firecracker has different colored leaves and they do not have the lobe at the bottom of the upper leaves. Both are real eyecatchers.
Date_____Location_____

Beard-tongue
Penstemon grinnellii

Fls.: Purple, tubular flower, up to 1 1/4 inch long and 3/4 inch across, lower lip has 3 prominent lobes with the middle lobe like a tongue. **Ht.:** 8 to 40 inches. **Lvs.:** Opposite, light green, saw-toothed edges. **Areas:** IV,IX,X. Blooms late in the season.
Date_____Location_____

Pine Penstemon
(Foothill Penstemon)
Penstemon heterophyllus

Fls.: Pairs of blue-violet, tubular, 2-lipped, 1 to 1 1/4 inch long flowers in a raceme. Under flowers are pairs of small leaves. **Ht.:** In clumps, 12 to 20 inches high. **Lvs.:** Narrow leaves up to 2 inches long in clusters around stalk, somewhat woody at base. **Areas:** IX,X. Blooms late in the season. Usually only part of the stalk is in bloom at any one time.
Date_____Location_____

Whorl-Leaf Penstemon
Keckiella ternata
Fls.: Scarlet, 2-lipped, narrow, tubular, up to 1 1/4 inches long. **Ht.:** up to 5 feet, straggly shrub. **Lvs.:** Narrow, pointed, up to 2 inches long, in whorls of 3 around the stalk. **Areas:** IV,IX,X. A similar shrub growing in lower elevations is the Heart-Leaved Penstemon (Penstemon cordifolius), except that it has opposite heart shaped leaves.
Date_____Location_____

X. 5 UNITED PETALS WITH A REGULAR SHAPE

A. MILKWEED FAMILY (Asclepiadaceae)
Named for its thick, milky sap. Unique flower with 5 swept-back petals surrounding a cup that sometimes has a curved horn growing from the center.

Rosy Milkweed
Asclepias californica
Fls.: Complicated structure. 5 cream-colored petals on yarnlike stems. In the center of the petals is a fleshy column on which are attached 5 maroon-colored "hoods" that contain a waxy mass. **Ht.:** 1 to 3 feet. **Lvs.:** Large wooly leaves, opposite, on a thick wooly stalk. **Areas:** VI,VIII,X. Large horn-shaped seedpods contain many silken-tufted seeds which blow in the wind when the pods open.
Date_____Location_____

Narrow-leaved Milkweed
Asclepias fascicularis
Fls.: Greenish-white and lavender tinted, in an umbel, typical milkweed flower with a horn. **Ht.:** 2 to 4 feet. **Lvs.:** 1 1/2 to 5 inches long in whorls of 3 to 6, many stalks from base. **Areas:** IX. The seedpod is narrow and sharply pointed, 2 to 3 1/2 inches long. It opens on the side when mature. Indians ground parched seeds and used them in their pinole (mush). The leaves were eaten as greens after the poisonous raw sap was washed out; the sap was cooked until congealed to remove the poison, washed in cold water to remove the bitter taste and was sometimes mixed with fat and chewed as gum. The fiber in the stalks was used to make cord or rope.
Date_____Location_____

Desert Milkweed
Asclepias erosa
Fls.: Wooly, 5-lobed, greenish-white, in umbels; between petals and stamens is a crown with 5 hooklike lobes. **Ht.:** Up to 3 feet. **Lvs.:** Opposite, somewhat leathery, spadelike, 3 to 6 inches long, few stalks from base, young stalks and leaves tend to be hairy, smoothing out with age. **Areas:** VI,VIII. Blooms late in the season.
Date_____Location_____

B. BORAGE OR FORGET-ME-NOT FAMILY (Boraginaceae)
Bristly herbs similar to the Phacelia or Waterleaf family in that the small 5-petaled, tubelike flowers grow on a coiled "stem." The chief difference is the 1 to 4 small, hard nutlets produced by each flower. Stamens are alternate with the petals and arise from partway up the flower tube. Leaves usually alternate.

Fiddleneck
Amsinckia tessellata
Fls.: Tiny yellow-orange flowers grow on a hairy, weak stalk; **Ht.:** up to 2 feet. **Lvs.:** Wavy, lancelike, with stiff hairs. **Areas:** All. The common name comes the way opening flower heads uncurl, resembling the neck of a violin just as do the Forget-Me-Not and the Phacelias. So how do you tell them apart? Well, this one is yellow and unfriendly looking. Those hairs on the stalk get awfully stickery as it matures. The nutlets (seeds) cause cirrhosis in cattle and horses.
Date_____Location_____

Forget-Me-Not
(Popcorn flower)
Cryptantha

Fls.: Tiny 5-petaled, tubelike flowers grow on a coiled stem, stamens are alternate to the petals. **Ht.:** Up to 2 feet. **Lvs.:** Long, narrow usually covered with white hairs. **Areas:** I,II, III,IV,VIII,IX,X,XII,XIV. Produces 4 hard nutlets. Over the area there are as many as 7 species of this flower, having only small differences. All of them are referred to as a Forget-Me-Not. It takes a botanist with a microscope to tell the difference between them. Although it is easy to see why some people refer to these flowers as Popcorn Flowers, the true Popcorn Flower is a different genus (Plagiobothrys nothofulvus), and is more rare although it can be found in Pine Canyon. We do have a Forget-Me-Not (C. micrantha), with purple dye in the roots which is confused with the Popcorn Flower. Indians used both plants to make a dye.
Date_____Location_____

Western Forget-Me-Not
Cryptantha circumscissa

Fls.: Tiny, white, in compact coil. **Ht.:** Up to 4 inches, rounded, spreading. **Lvs.:** Narrow, oblong, hairy, up to 5/8 inch long. **Areas:** I, IV, VIII, IX, X, XIV, in sandy soil. This is one Cryptantha flower-watchers can easily identify because it is so small.
Date_____Location_____

Chinese Pusley
(Wild Heliotrope, Salt Heliotrope, Quail Plant)
Heliotropium curassavicum

Fls.: Tiny, tubular, white with a yellow spot in the throat, fades to pale lilac, on long spikes with a slight curl, mostly in pairs. **Ht.:** 6 to 18 inches, spreading, with 4 to 20 inch long branches. **Lvs.:** Alternate, slightly succulent, oblong, 3/8 to 1 1/2 inches long. **Areas:** VI,VIII. Common roadside flower in moist, alkaline areas. Blooms from May to first frost. Indians dried the roots and ground them into a powder used to treat wounds.
Date_____Location_____

C. WATERLEAF FAMILY (Hydrophyllaceae)
Description much like the Forget-Me-Not family, except that these flowers have much longer, whiskerlike stamens and do not produce the nutlets.

Fremont Phacelia
(Yellow Throats)
Phacelia fremontii

Fls.: Bright blue to lavender with yellow throats, up to 3/4 inch in diameter, the curling pod typical of most phacelias is much less noticeable. **Ht.:** 6 to 12 inches. **Lvs.:** Small, thick, pinnately compound. **Areas:** IV,VI, VII,XII. May grow in masses so thick that it is difficult to see the leaves. In dry years one may find only a solitary plant here and there. This is another one of those problem flowers that often photographs pink instead of its true color.
Date_____Location_____

Lacy Phacelia
(Fern-leaved Phacelia, Tansy Phacelia)
Phacelia tanacetifolia

Fls.: Tiny blue or lavender flowers grow from curling pods at ends of stalk. **Ht.:** 8 to 32 inches. **Lvs.:** Heavily notched, fernlike leaves grow alternately on a stem from the main stalk; both stalk and leaves are covered with stiff hairs; bushy plant. **Areas:** Widespread but especially in I,II,III,XII,XIV. Likes to grow at the base of the Creosote Bush or other desert shrubs as well as together with poppies and coreopsis. Very fragrant.
Date_____Location_____

Whispering Bells
(California Yellow Bells)
Emmenanthe penduliflora

Fls.: Pale yellow, hanging, bell shaped. **Ht.:** 4 to 20 inches. **Lvs.:** Long and noticeably notched. **Areas:** VIII. The name refers to the soft rustling sound made by the breezes blowing the dried blossoms.
Date_____Location_____

Purple Mat
Nama demissum

Fls.: Many tiny, tubular flowers grow very close together on a low, spreading plant. **Ht.:** 2 to 3 inches. **Lvs.:** Tiny, narrow, just beneath the flower. **Areas:** II,IV,VI,XI. Grows with other "belly flowers" such as the Wallace Eriophyllum as well as the Dune Primrose. Jane Pinheiro's description of this one is, "Another dweller under the Joshua Trees is the creeping Purple Mat,... sometimes a single flower surmounting two green leaves less than half an inch over all, and sometimes a mat six or eight inches across, and an inch or so high. The little tube shaped blossoms are deep pink to purplish and occasionally white in color... [It] is the showiest of the ground clinging plants ... The plant's stems are brownish and the elongated leaves are bright blue-green. The flowers grow singly at the leaf terminals along the sprawling stems or in clusters at the stem terminals and are jewel like in their brilliance of color."
Date_____Location_____

Baby Blue Eyes
Nemophila menziesii

Fls.: Bright blue with white centers, bowl or saucer-shaped, 1/2 to 3/4 inch in diameter. **Ht.:** 4 to 14 inches. **Lvs.:** Many-branched plant with 5-lobed leaves, narrow at base, opposite, about 1 to 2 inches long. **Areas:** VII,IX,X,XII,XIV. Generally grows in moist places among Miner's Lettuce. Can be quite variable. On Tehachapi Willow Springs Road, Baby Blue Eyes may be seen on the open hillsides, never more than 6 inches high with flowers up to 1 1/2 inches in diameter on a single stalk. On Munz Ranch Road near Lake Elizabeth as well as many other places, Baby Blue Eyes can be found with many small, blue flowers growing on a bushy, thin-stemmed plant. At times a similar pale one may be found under Juniper Trees.
Date_____Location_____

Thickleaf Yerba Santa
Eriodictyon crassifolium

Fls.: Large bunches of 3/4 inch, funnel-shaped, light blue to lavender flowers at ends of sturdy branches. **Ht.:** 3 to 12 feet. **Lvs.:** Thick, lancelike, gray-green, 2 to 6 inches long and 1/2 to 2 inches wide. **Areas:** V,VII,VIII,IX,XIV. Yerba Santa means "holy herb" and was used by the mission fathers as a treatment for colds and other respiratory problems. The leathery leaves were also used in poultices for treatment of external bruises. Flowers photograph a reddish-purple.
Date_____Location_____

Sticky-leaved Yerba Santa
Eriodictyon trichocalyx
Fls.: White, funnel-shaped, up to 1/2 inch, in bunches. **Ht.:** Broad shrub, less than 5 feet high. **Lvs.:** Shiny, sticky, green, lancelike. **Areas:** IV,X. Most likely in Big Rock Creek area.
Date_____Location_____

Poodle Dog Bush
Turricula parryi

Fls.: Blue, funnel-shaped, on a coiled stem, ascending up top third of stalk. **Ht.:** 3 to 8 feet. **Lvs.:** Sticky, green, up to 6 inches long and narrow, about two thirds of the way up the stalk. **Areas:** Occasionally in Bouquet Canyon, but mainly in the high mountains, such as on Angeles Crest Highway. Causes dermatitis for some people. The reason for the common name is that, after the flowers go to seed the leaves fold back on the stalk, making a collar like that of a poodle dog. Flowers have a very foul odor.
Date_____Location_____

D. PHLOX FAMILY (Polemoniaceae)
Marked by a pattern of fives: 5 petals, 5 stamens and so on. Pinwheel or trumpetlike flower tube. Stamens are alternate to the petals and arise from near the top of the flower tube. The style splits into 3 at the tip.

Desert Calico
(Desert Butterflies)
Langloisia matthewsii

Fls.: Tiny flowers cover most of the small plant; 4 petals point up, one down, each of the top petals is colored white near the stamen, then red, then purple or lilac at the tips. **Ht.:** Compact plant, up to 3 inches. **Lvs.:** Tiny, wooly, bristly. **Areas:** IV,VI. Jane Pinheiro writes, that these "fuzzy, compact mounds of flowers sometimes cover the sands with a tiny pattern like old fashioned calico.... Each short reddish or brownish woody stem, terminates in a head of gray-green leaves and funny little blossoms, that do resemble butterflies hovering over the plant.... There may be hundreds of these dainty flowers on a very large specimen that is perhaps three inches high and eight inches across or there may be only four or five blossoms on a tiny plant the size of a thimble."
Date_____Location_____

Mustang Clover
Linanthus breviculus

Fls.: Deep pink to white, cluster of flowers is at the top of the thread-like stalk. **Ht.:** 2 to 10 inches. **Lvs.:** In tuffs along stalk. The largest group of leaves is at the point where the stems branch from the stalk. **Areas:** IV,XIV. Usually seen in moderately sized, homogenous groups.
Date_____Location_____

Davy Gilia,
(Birdseye Gilia, Tricolor Gilia)
Gilia latiflora ssp. davyi

Fls.: A large field of these flowers appears to be quite blue; an examination of the flower shows it to be blue on the tips and on the outside of the petals, pink or red inside and white on the lower petals with dark throats. **Ht.:** 8 to 14 inches. **Lvs.:** Basal, notched, several branches from base. **Areas:** IV, VI, VII, X, XII, XIII, XIV. This and several similar species are widespread throughout the Valley, some years. Dr. Bob Gustafson of the Los Angeles Natural History Museum comments, "The Gilias are probably the most difficult group of plants in the California flora to identify. Quite often they have to be sent to an expert on that genus to name." For this reason most of us common flower-watchers may want to be content with calling these fields of flowers Davy Gilia or, as many local people refer to them, Birdseye Gilia. Although it is probable that the real Birdseye Gilia, which has three dark spots in the throat, does not grow locally.

Date_____Location_____

Globe Gilia
Gilia capitata

Fls.: A compact ball (3/4 to 1 1/2 inches in diameter) of tiny, 5-petaled blue flowers at the end of a thin stalk. **Ht.:** 6 to 24 inches. **Lvs.:** Compound leaf growing mostly on lower portion of plant; heavily notched. **Areas:** II, VIII, X, XII, XIV ,XV. A very striking roadside flower growing in small groups along with Poppies, Lupine, and Coreopsis. Luiseno Indians parched the seeds, ground them and made a mush. Nevada Shoshone Indians made a tea from the whole plant as a treatment for children's colds.

Date_____Location_____

Golden Gilia
(Desert Gold)
Linanthus aureus
Fls.: Beautiful pure yellow, funnel-shaped, with orange to brownish-purple throat. **Ht.:** 2 to 6 inches. **Lvs.:** Short, thin, in bunches where stalk branches. **Areas:** XIV. Among Joshua Trees in large groups.
Date_____Location_____

Parry Gilia
(Fairy Bouttoniers)
Linanthus parryae
Fls.: Bunches of snow white, blue, or bluish-purple, 5-petaled flowers that are usually larger than the plant. **Ht.:** Rarely over 2 inches. **Lvs.:** Short, stiff, prickly. **Areas:** IV,VIII,X,XI,XIV,XV. The white ones sometimes are found with the blue or bluish-purple Parry Gila but when found alone in large groups, they may look like snow on the ground. Jane Pinheiro calls them "bouttoniers...of pink, and lavender-blue, and white Parry Gilia.... Sometimes it seems as though some jesting sprite had strewn the ground with flowers as it danced through the forest in the moonlight, for here is one, there a cluster, over yonder a long drift, and again, a solid patch of these fragile, pert little white, pink or lavender-blue flowers, set tight to the ground, apparently without any foliage at all.... At times one sees what appears to be a plant bearing pink, and lavender, and white blossoms all at once. This is merely another jest of nature, she having caused several plants to grow in such close proximity as to appear one." These are truly some of the most beautiful "belly flowers."
Date_____Location_____

Blue Mantle
Eriastrum diffusum
Fls.: Tiny pale blue, tubular flowers form clusters at ends of threadlike stems. **Ht.:** 1 to 6 inches. **Lvs.:** Narrow, short, bristly. **Areas:** II. Grows late in the season. May cover large areas among desert shrubs.
Date_____Location_____

Mesa Phlox
Eriastrum densifolium

Fls.: Electric blue, trumpet-shaped flowers form clusters on ends of woody stems. **Ht.:** 6 to 24 inches. **Lvs.:** Stiff, prickly, on somewhat bushy plant. **Areas:** IV,V,VII,X. In June when most flowers have dried and gone to seed and the ground is powdery dry, it is quite startling to round a bend in the road and come upon patches of these strikingly beautiful flowers.
Date_____Location_____

Rock Phacelia
(Wooly Britches)
Phacelia imbricata

Fls.: Tight, hairy coils of tubular or bell-shaped, white flowers. **Ht.:** 8 to 16 inches, in clumps. **Lvs.:** Large, alternate, mostly basal, rough, hairy, gray-green, spear-shaped, on stems. **Areas:** X. Not a very pretty flower.
Date_____Location_____

Evening Snow
(Desert Snow)
Linanthus dichotomus

Fls.: Funnel-shaped, 5-lobed, snow white with some purple in the lobes, opening in the evening and blooming until daylight. **Ht.:** 2 to 8 inches. **Lvs.:** Narrow, tiny on a threadlike stem. **Areas:** I,VIII,X,XII. As to this flower, Jane Pinheiro writes, "There is one small open meadow I often go by ... just to see re-enacted the miracle of Desert Snow.... It happens each evening in May or June, just as the sun is gathering up its last long rays for its nightly plunge behind the mountains. The dry sandy stretch on which some grass and other things are turning brown, suddenly, as one watches, becomes studded with shining white stars an inch or more across, and a jasmine like perfume is wafted into the evening air. Sometimes the blossoms jostle each other so closely as to almost cover the ground as with virgin snow flakes, hence the name Desert Snow. With the sun's rise the snow flakes vanish and one must look closely to find the tiny tubes of the furled blossoms which are so camouflaged as to blend perfectly with the ground."
Date_____Location_____

E. MORNING GLORY FAMILY (Convolvulaceae)

The flower is in a pattern of five's and bell-like. The buds are noticeably twisted. The stamens are alternate to the petals. This plant is usually a vine and sometimes has milky sap.

Bindweed (alien)
(Wild Morning Glory)
Convolvulus arvensis

Fls.: White with some pink, funnel-shaped, 1/2 to 1 1/2 inches across on trailing stems. **Ht.:** Trailing vine, usually on the ground, maybe 6 inches high, in colonies. **Lvs.:** Arrowhead shaped leaves with sharp lobes. **Areas:** Widespread in disturbed places such as roadsides, and farmer's fields. This is a weed with deep roots that is difficult to eradicate. New plants may develop from a network of roots, especially when these roots are cut or damaged, or from seeds that may lie dormant for several years.

Date_____Location_____

California Dodder
(Witches Hair, Devil's Hair, Strangle Weed,
Love Vine, Golden Thread)
Cuscuta californica

Fls.: Tiny, white, tubular, densely clustered; produces tiny flat seeds. **Ht.:** Depends upon height of shrub on which it grows. **Lvs.:** None. This plant is a showy, thin, orange vine that spreads its golden tangle over shrubs. **Areas:** Widespread. This is a parasitic plant without chlorophyll. The seeds germinate in the ground and the plant depends upon the food stored in the seed until it can attach itself to the host plant. It then severs its attachment to the ground and depends upon the host plant for its nourishment. California Buckwheat is a favorite host plant.

Date_____Location_____

F. HEATH FAMILY (Ericaceae)

Flowers are regular and symmetrical with 4 or 5 lobes or petals. Most have flowers that resemble upside down grecian urns. These trees, shrubs and somewhat woody herbs are usually evergreen.

Bigberry Manzanita
Arctostaphylos glauca

Fls.: Clusters of tiny white, upside down, urn-shaped flowers on nodding red stems. Flowers have shades of pink and a subtle fragrance. **Ht.:** Large shrub or small tree, 6 to 16 feet. **Lvs.:** Evergreen, oval, gray-green, brittle, 3/4 to 1 1/2 inches long on smooth, deep wine- colored, very crooked branches and trunk. **Areas:** All of the foothill and mountain areas to the south and west of the Antelope Valley. Although the flowers are truly beautiful, the most striking feature about this plant is the coloration of the trunk and limbs. *Manzanita* means "little apples" in Spanish and refers to the small red fruit.
Date_____Location_____

G. NIGHTSHADE FAMILY (Solanaceae)
Flower is in a pattern of five's and may be like a funnel, trumpet or a flattened star with a small protruding beak, in the center. Leaves are alternate. This very large family includes potatoes and tomatoes. Some parts of most of these plants are poisonous.

Purple Nightshade
Solanum xanti

Fls.: Many purple, starlike, fused-petal flowers with a prominent, bright yellow center on a very bushy plant. **Ht.:** 6 to 30 inches. **Lvs.:** Small, crinkled, spade-like. **Areas:** IV,VIII,X,XIV. Flower is similar to that of a potato plant.
Date_____Location_____

Desert Tobacco
Nicotiana bigelovii or trigonophylla

Fls.: Greenish-white, very long, tubular, with 5 sharp, pointed lobes. **Ht.:** 5 to 32 inches. **Lvs.:** Sticky, covered with hairs, lancelike, lower leaves have stems, upper leaves clasp the stalk. **Areas:** I,II,III,IV. Indians did smoke the leaves.
Date_____Location_____

Jimson Weed
(Sacred Datura, Thornapple)
Datura meteloides

Fls.: Large, bell-shaped, white turning to purple as the flowers fold up; blooms all night until mid-morning. **Ht.:** Spreading bush, up to 40 inches high. **Lvs.:** Gray, broad, shovel-shaped, 1 1/2 to 5 inches long. **Areas:** Very widespread over most of the Antelope Valley. To some people this is simply a beautiful flower, to others it is a noxious, poisonous weed, but to the Southwest Indians, this holy plant was to be used in religious and puberty rites. This was the "Cult of the Toloache." The powered root mixed with water causes hallucinations, deemed by the Indians to be a religious experience, lasting for about 3 days. Some Mexican peasants believed that eating a few seeds made them clairvoyant so that they could find lost burros and even fortell the future.
Date_____Location_____

Anderson Thorn
(Box Thorn)
Lycium andersonii

Fls.: White-lavender fading to white, solitary or in pairs, funnel-shaped, with 4 or 5 lobes. **Ht.:** 1 1/2 to 9 feet. **Lvs.:** Green, fleshy, up to 5/8 inch long, hangs in bunches from white branches. **Areas:** I,VI,VIII. Fruit is red and elliptical, has many seeds, and is up to 5/8 inch long. This shrub has sharp, needle-like thorns.
Date_____Location_____

Peach Thorn
Lycium cooperi

Fls.: Greenish-white with lavender veins, up to 9/16 inch long, tubular, with lobes 1/2 as long as the tube, in bunches with stems and leaves. **Ht.:** 2 to 6 feet. **Lvs.:** Green, oblong, up to 1 1/4 inch long, in bunches with the flowers. **Areas:** I,VI,VIII. Fruit is green. Seeds are in two compartments. A unique groove circles the fruit near the top. Thorns are short and thick, up to 3/8 inch.
Date_____Location_____

H. CUCUMBER OR GOURD FAMILY (Cucurbitaceae)

Vines which may or may not have tendrils (a slender, curled stem growing from the main vine which aids in holding onto support material). Sometimes has a squashlike blossom. Produces a melonlike fruit. Family includes squash and cucumbers besides gourds.

Calabazilla

(Buffalo Gourd, Coyote Gourd, Coyote Melon, Chilicoyote, Chilicoyote, Mock Orange)

Cucurbita foetidissima

Fls.: Yellow, tubular, 3 or 4 inches long, like a squash blossom; produces a yellow gourd with a smooth, hard rind, 2 to 3 inches in diameter. **Ht.:** Coarse, heavy vine, trailing along the ground, covering an area up to 500 square feet or more. **Lvs.:** Triangular, greenish-gray, 6 to 12 inches long. **Areas:** VII,X,XII. The common names, Coyote Gourd, Coyote Melon and Chilicoyote, apparently come from some Indian's disdain for the coyote, saying that only a coyote would be dumb enough to eat it. Mock Orange refers to the appearance of the gourds lying on the ground after a frost kills the vine.

Date_____Location_____

Wild Cucumber

(Common Man Root, Old Man in the Ground)

Marah horridus

Fls.: White or cream, 5-pointed star, about 1/2 inch in diameter; male flowers number from 5 to 12 in a raceme; female flowers are single on the end of a small, green, very thorny fruit which is 3 1/2 to 6 inches long and 2 to 3 inches in diameter at maturity. While green, the fruit forms holes at the bottom end. As the seeds mature, they fall to the ground through these holes. **Ht.:** Climbs on other plants. Runners may be up to 10 feet long. **Lvs.:** 5-pointed, deeply lobed, green leaf, 2 to 3 inches in diameter. **Areas:** Foothill areas surrounding the Antelope Valley with the most likely location being Bouquet Canyon. I have found no explanation for the common name "Wild Cucumber," but the other two common names refer to the enormous size of the root, which may be 6 feet long and 18 inches to 2 feet in diameter. The botanical name Marah comes from the Old Testament, (Exodus 15:22-26), "And when they came to Marah, they could not drink of the waters of Marah, for they were bitter: therefore the name of it was called Marah." The juice of the root is bitter and was used in an alcoholic drink referred to as "Stoughton's Bitters," advertised as "The Bitters that won the West."

Date_____Location_____

I. HONEYSUCKLE FAMILY (Caprifoliaceae)

Small trees, shrubs or vines with long-funnel like flowers growing in pairs with 4 stamens, 5 petals and 5 sepals. Leaves opposite. The most common members of this family in Antelope Valley are the Elderberry Tree and a Wild Honeysuckle growing in the chaparral.

Elderberry Tree
Sambucus mexicana

Fls.: Tiny, creamy yellow flowers growing in an umbel, up to 5 inches in diameter; berries are blue or white, covered by a white powdery substance. **Ht.:** Small trees or large shrubs up to 12 feet. **Lvs.:** Glossy; 2 to 4 inches; wavy, serrated edges. **Areas:** IV,VII,VIII,IX,X,XV. Berries are used to make jelly or wine. Botanical name Sambucus comes from the Greek word sambuke, the name of a musical instrument made of elder wood.

Date_____Location_____

XI. SEVERAL APPARENT PETALS WITH A CONE CENTER

A. LIZARD TAIL FAMILY (Saururaceae)

Only one member of this family is prominent in Antelope Valley and is described below.

Yerba Mansa
Anemopsis californica

Fls.: The 5 to 8 white, apparent petals around a 1/2 to 1 1/2 inches cone are actually modified bracts, the actual flowers are minute, without sepals or petals, sunk in the cone. **Ht.:** Up to 2 feet. **Lvs.:** Elliptic, oblong, dark green, 2 to 10 inches long. Most grow from the base, but under each flower head is a leaf clasping the stem with another leaf growing from that joint. **Areas:** IV. The most spectular display is at Barrel Springs. Grows in wet, alkaline areas. To the Spanish this was the "herb of the tamed indian." (Mansa means "tame or mild" in Spanish.) The root has a spicy smell, and a peppery taste and had many medicinal uses, as a blood purifier, for rheumatism, and to reduce swellings. The powdered root was used on sores.

Date_____Location_____

XII. MANY APPARENT PETALS AND MANY APPARENT STAMENS

A. SUNFLOWER OR COMPOSITE FAMILY (Asteraceae)   This is by far the largest flower family with about 850 species in California. The flower head actually is made up of many flowers. The apparent "petals" are called ray flowers and the apparent "stamens" are called cone or disk flowers. Some flowers may only have ray flowers (dandelions) where others have only disk flowers (thistles), but most of the plants in this family have both.

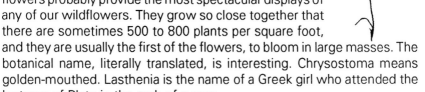

Common Sunflower
(Compass Plant)
Helianthus annuus

Fls.: Classical sunflower head of bright yellow ray flowers and tubular brownish disk flowers, 3 to 5 inches across. **Ht.:** 6 feet or more. **Lvs.:** Alternate, oval-shaped up to 10 inches long with sandpaperery texture created by stiff hairs; stalk is rough, sturdy and fibrous. **Areas:** Widespread, especially in VIII,X,XI,XII,XIII,XV. The Kansas state flower has spread to the grain fields and roadsides of the Antelope Valley as a common weed. The name "Compass Plant" refers to the north-south direction in which the leaves tend to point.

Date_____Location_____

Goldfields
Lasthenia chrysostoma

Fls.: Ray flowers are pale yellow on the tips and a deeper yellow next to the deep yellow cone flowers. **Ht.:** 4 to 8 inches. **Lvs.:** Narrow, opposite. **Areas:** VII (beside the Antelope Valley Freeway in Palmdale), VIII,X,XII,XIII as well as on 60th St. West near Avenues I and H. Next to the California Poppy and the Coreopsis, these very fragrant flowers probably provide the most spectacular displays of any of our wildflowers. They grow so close together that there are sometimes 500 to 800 plants per square foot, and they are usually the first of the flowers, to bloom in large masses. The botanical name, literally translated, is interesting. Chrysostoma means golden-mouthed. Lasthenia is the name of a Greek girl who attended the lectures of Plato in the garb of a man.

Date_____Location_____

Bigelow Coreopsis
Coreopsis bigelovii

Fls.: Ray flowers are of 2 yellow tones with the deeper yellow being closest to the deep yellow cone flowers. **Ht.:** 12 to 20 inches. **Lvs.:** Mostly basal with naked stems. **Areas:** VIII,X,XII,XIII, XV. In great profusion. The name "Coreopsis" comes from the Greek word meaning "resembling a bug or a tick," which refers to the structure underneath the petals. Another common name, which is rarely used now, is Tickseed.

Date_____Location_____

California Coreopsis
Coreopsis californica

Fls.: Solid yellow ray flowers with nearly square outside edges, slightly deeper yellow cone flowers. **Ht.:** 6 to 14 inches. **Lvs.:** Basal and thread-like. **Areas:** II,III,IV. In great profusion near the Indian Museum. Sometimes grows in soil as hard as a brick. There are other species of Coreopsis (*C. calliopsidea* and *C. douglasii*) that have very similar characteristics to the two listed.

Date_____Location_____

Monolopia
(Hilltop Daisy, Wooly Daisy)
Monolopia lanceolata

Fls.: 2 toned yellow ray flowers with a "V" in the outer edge. Outer portion of the ray flowers turns white with age, cone flowers are a deep yellow. **Ht.:** Usually 6 to 14 inches but during March 1978 nature put on the most remarkable display of Monolopia on the hills just north of Bacchus Road. The Monolopia were over two feet tall and grew so close together that all you could see were blossoms. **Lvs.:** Lancelike growing up the flower stalks, which are covered with white hairs. **Areas:** I,XII. Fields of these flowers can be mistaken for the Coreopsis at a distance. However, the white hairs or wool that covers the plant gives the fields a creamy yellow appearance. The stalk is much sturdier than the Coreopsis and branches freely.

Date_____Location_____

Sunflower

Balsam Root
(Deltoid Balsamroot)
Balsamorhiza deltoidea

Fls.: Deep yellow ray flowers; deep yellow, ragged cone flowers turning brown with maturity; flower head up to 4 inches in diameter. **Ht.**: Up to 3 feet. **Lvs.**: Very large, nearly smooth, wavy, arrow-shaped leaves grow from basal clump. **Areas:** IX,XIII. Grows on hillsides in moderately sized colonies.
Date_____Location_____

Tidy Tips
(Two-Toned Tidy Tips)
Layia platyglossa

Fls.: Ray flowers are yellow with white tips, with 3 points on outer edge; cone flowers are deep yellow. **Ht.**: 4 to 12 inches. **Lvs.**: Variable. Basal leaves are coarsely saw-toothed while upper leaves are lancelike and alternate. **Areas:** VII,VIII,XIII. Some years, when the rains are plentiful, many acres of the Ana Verde Valley (just west of Palmdale) are carpeted with this two toned daisylike flower. Because of the foliage and the white tips on the ray flowers, fields of this flower appear from a distance, to be a cream color (even lighter than the Monolopia).
Date_____Location_____

Desert Tidy Tips
(White Daisy)
Layia glandulosa

Fls: Daisylike with 8 to 24 white ray flowers, three lobed at the tips. Many yellow cone flowers. Flower head is about 1 1/2 inches in diameter. **Ht.:** 4 to 16 inches. **Lvs.:** Alternate, with stiff hairs; note unique leaf structure in photocopy. **Areas:** II, IV, I, VIII, X, XII, XIII, XIV. Grows in among the desert shrubs in small groups.
Date_____Location_____

Fremont Pincushion
Chaenactis fremontii

Fls.: No ray flowers. The cone flower head has an outer row or two of scalloped flowers arranged like a double ruffle around a soft cushiony center that is smooth before the cone flowers open, but looks like it is full of pins when the narrow tubes elongate. Heads are roughly 1 to 1 1/2 inches in diameter. Color is creamy or off white. **Ht.:** 4 to 16 inches. **Lvs.:** Alternate, short, narrow, not too noticeable when flower is in bloom. **Areas:** Very widespread with a great many in areas I,II,VIII,X,XIV. Other Chaenactis that may be found in the Valley are the *C. macrantha*, with a somewhat fleshy or purple tone to the flower, and the *C. xantiana*, which is also white or somewhat flesh- toned.
Date_____Location_____

Yellow Pincushion
(Golden Girls, Common Yellow Chaenactis)
Chaenactis glabriuscula

Fls.: Very much like the Fremont Pincushion described above except that this one is very yellow. **Ht.:** 4 to 14 inches. **Lvs.:** Alternate, short, narrow. **Areas:** I,IV,X,XI,XII,XIV. Of these Jane Pinheiro says, "The most showy of these [Pincushions] is Golden Girls...whose coarse, fernlike, gray green foliage serves as a charming background for the lovely bright yellow 'cushions' that are pierced with many deeper yellow 'pins'."
Date_____Location_____

Wallace Eriophyllum
Eriophyllum wallacei

Fls.: Small, deep yellow ray flowers with square tips; deeper yellow cone flowers. **Ht.:** Usually less than 2 inches, a "belly flower." **Lvs.:** Wooly, short. **Areas:** II,III,IV,V,XII. Grows in gravelly, sandy soil. May be a solitary plant with one flower head or may have many branches with many flower heads. A similar plant, E. pringlei or Wooly Eriophyllum, can be distinguished by the tuffs of "cotton" around the flower heads. Also E. pringlei has only cone flowers.
Date_____Location_____

Golden Yarrow
(Long Stemmed Eriophyllum)
Eriophyllum confertiflorum

Fls.: Short, deep yellow ray flowers; golden cone flowers in a cluster at the ends of the stalks. **Ht.:** up to 18 inches. **Lvs.:** Thin, alternate, gray-green on white, wooly branches. **Areas:** IV,VII,VIII,IX, XIII as well as the high mountains. The common name is misleading in that it is not a Yarrow, but the flower heads may resemble the Yarrow.
Date_____Location_____

Autumn Vinegar Weed
Lessingia lemmonii peirsonii

Fls.: Tiny tufts of yellow flowers on ends of a much-branched plant that when squeezed, give off a strong sour, resinous odor. **Ht.:** 4 to 18 inches. **Lvs.:** Tiny, narrow, green leaves thoughout the plant. **Areas:** IV,X. In spite of its name this plant does begin blooming in late May or early June and blooms all summer.
Date_____Location_____

Desert Dandelion
Malacothrix glabrata

Fls.: Has ray flowers only. Yellow centers fade to white on the outer edges. On single hollow stems. **Ht.:** 4 to 18 inches. **Lvs.:** Basal, narrow, with narrow lobes. **Areas:** This is one of the most widespread flowers in the Antelope Valley. Great fields of Dandelion may be seen from Bacchus Road to Fort Tejon Road to Lancaster (where it still grows on vacant city blocks), to Ave. D and on to Fairmont Road. It is common for this flower to grow with a similar species, *M.californica*, in large fields. Both are usually referred to locally as Desert Dandelion. The difference is that the *M. californica* has a red or maroon-colored center and has a somewhat wooly appearance. Both have rounded, feathery seed heads similar to the dandelions that are such pests in lawns.
Date_____Location_____

Please note the following four flowers look very much like the Desert Dandelion in that they have only ray flowers and are roughly the same size.

Snake's Head
(Snakehead, Snake's Head Dandelion)
Malacothrix coulteri

This plant differs from the Desert Dandelion in that the leaves are not basal and are broader. The name comes from the overlapping scales on the rounded, unopened flower bud.

Date_____Location_____

Silver Puff
Microseris linearifolia

Flower head is a ragged group of pale yellow ray flowers that bloom for a very brief period. Most noteable feature about plant is the coarse, round, silver ball of seeds which stays around for some time. Jane Pinheiro says the Silver Puff is "so named because the almost black seeds set off the silver of their downy wings to perfection. ... Often Silver Puffs are to be found in quite extensive colonies on open hillsides, though they sometimes invade the valley floor, where they are usually found singly."

Date_____Location_____

Scale Bud
Anisocoma acaulis

Identification points for this plant that separate it from the dandelion are the large, wooly, irregular, basal leaves and the bracts enclosing the bud, which are dotted and edged with red. The plant is two to eight inches high and is very common throughout the area.

Date_____Location_____

Yellow Tackstem
Calycoseris parryi

This dandelionlike plant grows from four to twelve inches high, has narrow, basal leaves and tack-shaped glands on the stems below the flower heads. Not common.

Date_____Location_____

145

Mojave Aster
Machaeranthera tortifolia
Fls.: Long, narrow, light to medium lavender ray flowers with deep yellow to orange disk flowers on a bushy plant. **Ht.:** 1 to 3 feet. **Lvs.:** Narrow lance-like with spiny teeth along edges, usually covered with gray hairs. **Areas:** I,II,III,IV and north of the Palmdale reservoir.
Date_____Location_____

Chicory (alien)
(Blue Sailors, Succory)
Cichorium intybus
Fls.: Bright blue ray flowers with a small center of yellow disk flowers scattered throughout a rangy plant; flowers close by 10:00 A.M. **Ht.:** Up to 4 feet. **Lvs.:** 3 to 8 inch basal leaves, heavily notched; upper leaves are much smaller, and have various shapes. **Areas:** VIII. Grows in large groups in wet meadows. This is a garden escapee from Asia. Chicory has been used as a vegetable and for medicinal purposes in Europe and Asia for centuries. The new leaves were cooked much like dandelions. Leaves were blanched and used as salad greens. But probably the best-known use is as a coffee additive or substitute. The large root is dug up, washed, cut into strips, and either roasted or dried in the open sun and ground to make the coffee additive. It has spread over most of the United States and is famous in Louisiana coffees.
Date_____Location_____

Desert Straw
(Desert Wirelettuce)
Stephanomeria pauciflora

Fls.: Small, pink to reddish, fade to a buff color, ray flowers only. **Ht.:** 6 to 14 inches. **Lvs.:** Tiny, narrow, bluish-green, toothed lobes; leaves all but disappear when the plant is blooming; stalk and branches are bare and very tough. **Areas:** Widespread, but never in any large groups. This is a strange little plant that for much of the year looks like straw. In the spring, it becomes green, sprouts a few leaves and then puts out a flower here and there. It is one of those flowers which is not showy. When a flower-watcher comes upon it, the common response is, "What in the world is that strange plant?" It is reported to be a favorite food of burros and bighorn sheep.
Date_____Location_____

Mojave Thistle
Cirsium mohavense

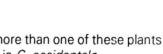

Lvs.: Disk flowers only in an extremely thorny pod. Varies in color from pink to bright red to purple. **Ht.:** 2 to 5 feet. **Lvs.:** 4 to 10 inches long, wooly, very thorny. **Areas:** IV,V,VII,VIII,IX,X,XIV. Rare to see more than one of these plants at a time. Another Thistle that is very similar is *C. occidentale*.
Date_____Location_____

Pearly Everlasting
Anaphalis margaritacea

Fls.: Flowers appear pearly white, whereas the cone flowers are actually yellow; they are almost completely covered with shiny pearly bracts that give the plant its common name. **Ht.:** 6 inches to 3 feet. **Lvs.:** Linear and alternate, tend to be hairy. **Areas:** VIII, IX, X. When grown on your own property, these may be picked and make wonderful straw flowers in a dry arrangement. The bracts will open and stiffen, giving the flower the look of a straw flower.
Date_____Location_____

Brittlebush
(Acton Encelia)
Encelia virginensis ssp. actoni

Fls.: 8 to 18 ragged, yellow, ray flowers with notches in the outer edges and a large group of yellow-orange cone flowers at the ends of 9 to 12 inch bare stems. **Ht.:** 2 to 4 feet. **Lvs.:** Deciduous, the immature green leaves quickly becoming gray, shovel-shaped, up to 1 1/2 inches long, not smooth. **Areas:** IV,VIII,XII,XIV. Blooms late in the season. When blooming, these bushes are full of 2 to 3-inch flowers and are quite showy. The most-used common name is incorrect in that the real Brittlebush (Encelia farinosa), grows in the Anza Borrego Desert.
Date_____Location_____

Linear-Leafed Goldenbush
(Narrowleaf Goldenbush)
Haplopappus linearifolius

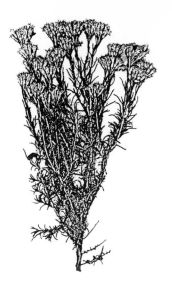

Fls.: 8 to 12 separate ray flowers, a relatively small center of cone flowers, both bright yellow on a green, 3 to 6 inch, bare stem, flowers cover bush. **Ht.:** A rounded, bushy shrub, 1 1/2 to 5 feet tall. **Lvs.:** Thick, narrow, green, up to 1 1/2 inches long, in great numbers on woody branches. **Areas:** IV, V, VII, VIII, IX, X, XII ,XIV, XV. The most common yellow sring- blooming shrub in the western Antelope Valley. The Haplopappus is a very large genera, with some 29 species and subspecies in Southern California as listed by Dr. Philip Munz.

Date_____Location_____

Cooper Goldenbush
Haplopappus cooperi

Fls.: 0, 1 or 2 yellow ray flowers; balance of the flower made up of cone flowers; short stems; more than one head on the end of a branch; flowers cover a rounded, many-branched bush. **Ht.:** 1 to 4 feet. **Lvs.:** Green, narrow, alternate. **Areas:** XIV.

Date_____Location_____

Cotton Thorn
(Shortspine, Horsebrush)
Tetradymia spinosa

Fls.: Yellow cone flowers only, coming out of 3/4 inch, greenish-gray pods; seeds are cotton balls that completely cover the plant once the flowers are gone. **Ht.:** 2 to 4 feet. **Lvs.:** Mostly gray, only slightly green, tiny, narrow, sparse on very thorny, white, rigid branches. **Areas:** IV,VII,VIII,XII,XIV. A very showy desert shrub both in bloom and in seed. The botanical name Tetradymia is from the Greek meaning "four together," referring to some species having heads of four flowers. The spines reportedly were used as tattoo needles by Native Americans.

Date_____Location_____

Great Basin Sage
(Basin Sagebrush)
Artemisia tridentata

Fls.: 4 to 6 tiny, rarely noticed cone flowers on a spike, no ray flowers. **Ht.:** Up to 15 feet. **Lvs.:** Narrow, gray or silver, very fragrant, (described by some as a terebinthine aroma or turpentine smell.) The tips of the leaves are "three toothed" leading to the species name tridentata. **Areas:** IV,VII,VIII,IX,X,XIII,XIV. Trunk and branches have shaggy bark. The common names of this shrub are misleading in that the sages are in the mint family whereas this one is in the sunflower family. The name was probably given because of its aromatic qualities.

Date_____Location_____

XIII. NUMEROUS PETALS IN A REGULAR SHAPE

A. CACTUS FAMILY (Cactaceae)
Mostly succulent, perennial plants having a large number of thorns or spines. Identity is often based on the arrangement of each spine cluster.

Silver Cholla
(Golden Cholla)
Opuntia echinocarpa

Fls.: Greenish-yellow, 1 1/4 to 2 1/2 inches across, 1 inch petals are at the ends of the branches. **Ht.:** 2 to 5 feet. **Lvs.:** 3/4 to 1 1/4 inch silver spines or needlelike thorns take the place of leaves. These are very thick over the entire plant. It has one trunk with many round branches. **Areas:** IV,V,VIII. Flowers are difficult to find in that they do not bloom each year and even then have only a few blossoms. Part of the year the spines look gold which is the reason for the other common name.

Date_____Location_____

Beavertail Cactus
Opuntia basilaris

Fls.: Showy, magenta, up to 3 inches across, yellow stamens, fruit and flowers grow at the top end of pads 5 to 10 inches long. **Ht.:** Up to 14 inches, clumps may be 2 feet across. **Lvs.:** None. No spines. Pads are covered with pockets of stickers. **Areas:** Widespread on the desert floor and up to 6,000 feet in elevation but rarely in large groups. The red or wine colored fruit was eaten by Indians and makes excellent jelly.

Date_____Location_____

INDEX
OF COMMON NAMES
Page numbers of photographs are in **bold** print.

Deer Weed, Broom	106,39	Golden Gilia	133,41
Desert Calico	131,56	Golden Girls	143,43
Desert Candle	97,48	Golden Mariposa Lily	19,34
Desert Dandelion	144,45	Golden Stars	21,35
Desert Mariposa	19,48	Golden Yarrow	144,45
Desert Milkweed	126,72	Goldfields	140,33,42
Desert Snow	134,71	Golondrina	13,64
Desert Straw	146,57	Greasewood	117,86
Desert Tidy Tips	142,72	Great Basin Sage	149,88
Desert Trumpet	16,34	Hairy Lotus	106,38
Dodder, California	135,92	Heliotrope, Wild	128,70
Dune Primrose	104,33,67	Heronsbill	112,55
Elderberry Tree	139,78	Hilltop Daisy	141,43
Elegant Lupine	108,52	Hoary Cress	98,66
Eriophyllum, Wallace	143,44	Hollyhock, Desert	111,40
Evening Snow	134,71	Hooker Primrose	103,38
Fairy Bouttoniers	133,61,71	Hop Sage	14,82
Fairy Trumpet	124,54	Horehound	120,70
Farewell to Spring	104,51	Horse Chestnut	31,79
Fiddleneck	127,41	Hyacinth, Wild	22,57
Filaree, Red Stem	112,55	Indian Paintbrush	122,54
Flannel Bush	15,73	Indian Pinks	116,53
Flattop Buckwheat	18,82	Indian Tea	12,78
Forget-Me-Not	127,70	Jewel Flower	96,50
Four O'Clock, Giant	100,68,50	Jimson Weed	137,88
Fremontia	15,73	Johnny Jump-up	110,40
Fremont Phacelia	128,61	Joshua Tree	22,74,75
Fremont Pincushion	143,72	Juniper, Calif.	12,73
Fringe Pod	97	Keel Fruit, Slender	96,37
Fringed Onion	21,49	Lg. Yellow Desert Primrose	103,38
Giant 4 O'Clock	100,50,68	Lacy Phacelia	129,60
Giant Blazing Star	118,39	Larkspur, Parish	113,59
Gilia, Davy	132,60	Larkspur, Scarlet	113,48
Gilia, Globe	132,60	Lilac, California	29,82
Gilia, Golden	133,41	Little Gold Poppy	27,35
Gilia, Parry	133,61,71	Live Forever	115,46
Globe Gilia	132,60	Loco Weed	106,39
Globemallow, Desert	111,40	Love Vine	135,92
Goldenbush, Cooper	148,91	Lupine	108,57
Goldenbush, Linear Leafed	148,91	Lupine, Adonis	109,58
Golden Cholla	149,94	Lupine, Bentham	109,58
Golden Ear Drops	27,35	Lupine, Bush	109,58

Lupine, Elegant	108,52	Pearly Everlasting	147,73
Lupine, Pygmy-Leaved	109,58	Pennyroyal	120,69
Lupine, Royal Desert	108,58	Penstemon, Pine	125,60
Lupine, White	110,68	Pepper Grass	31,36
Mallow, Apricot	111,40	Persian Prince	119,59
Mallow, Bush	111,85	Phacelia, Fremont	128,61
Man Root	138,94	Phacelia, Lacy	129,60
Manzanita, Bigberry	136,89	Pie Plant	16,46
Maroposa, Golden	19,34	Pincushion, Fremont	143,72
Mariposa, White	20,64	Pincushion, Yellow	143,43
Mesa Phlox	134,62	Pine Penstemon	125,60
Milkweed, Desert	126,72	Pin-Point Clover	107,52
Milkweed, Narrow-Leaved	126,71	Pipe Stem Clematis	114,93
Milkweed, Rosy	126,55	Poison Oak	115,84
Miner's Lettuce	110,69	Poodle Dog Bush	131,88
Mock Orange	138,93	Popcorn Flower	127,70
Mojave Aster	146,63	Poppy, Bush	28,82
Mojave Thistle	147,57	Poppy, Prickly	28.65
Monkey Flower, Bush	123,87	Prickly Poppy	28,65
Monkey Flower, Common	123,42	Primrose, Brown-Eyed	105,67
Monolopia	141,43	Primrose, Calif.	105,67
Mormon Tea	12,78	Primrose, Dune	104,33,67
Morning Glory, Wild	135,91	Primrose, Mustard-Like	102,37
Mountain Lilac	29,82	Primrose, Spencer	102,37
Mustang Clover	131,56	Prince's Plume	96,37
Mustard-Like Primrose	102,37	Punctured Bract	17,47
Mustard, Tumble	32,36	Purple Mat	129,56
Narrow Leaved Milkweed	126,71	Purple Nightshade	136,62
Old Man in the Ground	138,94	Purple Sage	121,84
Onion, Crested	22,65	Pygmy-Leaved Lupine	109,58
Onion, Fringed	21,49	Quixote Plant	24,76,77
Our Lord's Candle	24,76,77	Rattlesnake Weed	13,64
Owl's Clover	123,54	Rattleweed, Desert	107,51
Paintbrush, Indian	122,54	Red Maids	110,51
Paintbrush, Wooly	122,53	Red Ribbons	104,51
Paintbrush, Yellow	122,41	Red Stem Filaree	112,55
Palmer Mariposa	20,48	Rhubarb, Wil	d16,46
Paper Bag Bush	121,87	Rock Cress	97,50
Parish Larkspur	113,59	Rock Phacelia	134
Parry Gilia	133,61,71	Rose, Calif. Wild	116,86
Parsley, Wild	118,40	Rosy Milkweed	126,55
Peach Thorn	137,90	Royal Desert Lupine	108,58

Russian Thistle	14,**46**	Tidy Tips	142,**44**
Sacred Datura	137,**88**	Tidy Tips, Desert	142,**72**
Sage, Blue	121,**84**	Tobacco, Desert	136,**70**
Sage, Great Basin	149,**88**	Tree Poppy	28,**82**
Sage, Thistle	119,**59**	Tricolor Gilia	132,**60**
Sage, White	120,**68**	Tumble Mustard	32,**36**
Salt Cedar	30,**78**	Tumbleweed	14,**46**
Sand Mat	13,**64**	Turkish Rugging	17,**47**
Sand Verbena	100,**49**	Vinegar Weed, Autumn	144,**46**
Saucer Plant	17,**47**	Virgin's Bower	114,**93**
Scale Bud	145,**45**	Wallace Eriophyllum	143,**44**
Scarlet Bugler	125,**54**	Wallflower, Western	32,**36**
Scarlet Larkspur	113,**48**	Water Cress	98,**68**
Seepspring Monkey Flower	123,**42**	Western Forget-Me-Not	128,**69**
Shepherds Purse	98	Western Wallflower	32,**36**
Shield Cress	99,**66**	Whispering Bells	129,**41**
Silver Cholla	149,**94**	White Lupine	110,**68**
Silver Puff	145,**45**,**73**	White Mariposa	20,**64**
Skeleton Weed	17,**64**	White Sage	120,**68**
Slender Keel Fruit	96,**37**	Whorl- Leaf Penstemon	125,**87**
Slippery Elm	15,**73**	Wild Buckwheat	18,**79**
Snake's Head	145	Wild Cucumber	138,**94**
Soap Bush	29,**82**	Wild Hyacinth	22,**57**
Soap Plant	20,**63**	Wild Parsley	118,**40**
Sour Dock	17,**47**	Wild Rhubarb	16,**46**
Spectacle Pod	97,**66**	Wine Cups	103,**50**
Spencer Primrose	102,**37**	Winter Fat	15,**79**
Squaw Bush	114,**85**	Wishbone Bush	101,**49**
Squaw Cabbage	97,**48**	Witches Hair	135,**92**
Squaw Tea	12,**78**	Woody Bottlewasher	105,**66**
Sticky-leaved Yerba Santa	130,**89**	Wooly Blue Curls	121,**88**
Sticky Monkey Flower	123,**87**	Wooly Daisy	141,**43**
Suncups, Desert	102,**38**	Wooly Paintbrush	122,**53**
Sunflower, Common	140,**42**	Yellow Pincushion	143,**43**
Tamarisk, French	30,**78**	Yellow Tackstem	145
Tamarisk, Smallflower	30,**78**	Yellow Throats	128,**61**
Thickleaf Yerba Santa	130,**89**	Yellow Turban	16,**34**
Thistle, Mojave	147,**57**	Yerba Mansa	139,**72**
Thistle Sage	119,**59**	Yerba Santa, Sticky-leaved	130,**89**
Thorn, Anderson	137,**90**	Yerba Santa, Thickleaf	130,**89**
Thornapple	137,**88**	Yucca	24,**76**,**77**
Thorn, Cotton	148,**92**	Yucca Palm	22,**74**,**75**
Thorn, Peach	137,**90**	Zygadene, Desert	20,**63**

INDEX
OF BOTANICAL NAMES

FLOWER AREAS OF THE ANTELOPE VALLEY

In years when we have much rain between October and May and maybe a foot of snow without any hot, drying winds, the whole Valley becomes a veritable flower garden. But this happens only once in a lifetime. In most years when we have near average rainfall or better, certain areas of the Valley are more prone to have an abundance of wildflowers than others. These areas are listed below. **Also, please see map at the end of this section.**

Area I. BACCHUS ROAD

Some of the earliest blooms are usually found on the hills north of Bacchus Road and west of the freeway. (Bacchus Road is between Rosamond and Mojave.) The flowers most likely to be found here are fields of Coreopsis and Monolopia with a scattering of Phacelia, Little Gold Poppies, Blue Dicks and Forget-Me-Nots. Later in the season the desert floor south of the road is blanketed with Desert Dandelion and Mojave Aster as well as bunches of the Cream Cups with the butter yellow in the petals.

Area II. WILSONA (around 170th St. East and Ave. M)

In the early season one can usually find large colonies of yellow Pepper Grass growing on sandy dunes. Later large fields of Coreopsis can be seen (especially east of the Indian Museum and on Ave. H and 120th St. East), with Phacelia growing at the base of the desert shrubs. In the dry washes are large colonies of Wild Rhubarb. At Saddleback Buttes State Park (170th St. East and Ave. J), one might find in addition to the Coreopsis, fields of the Dune Primrose, Sand Verbena, Pincushion and Brown Eyed Primrose with an occasional Large Yellow Desert Primrose. Late in the season the very fragrant Pennyroyal can be found in profusion in the sandy areas of the park. Further east, around 180th St. East, are sometimes large fields of the Royal Desert Lupine, and Apricot Mallow as well as the Desert Candle.

Area III. HI VISTA (around 200th St. East and Ave. G)

This area is noted for a great variety of desert flowers and, in particular, the Desert Candle, which some years covers many acres of the desert floor along with large quantities of Goldfields, Lacy Phacelia, Mojave Asters and Fremont Phacelia.

Area IV. FORT TEJON ROAD (south of Pearblossom near Longview Road,) VALYERMO ROAD and BIG ROCK CREEK ROAD.

In addition to the fields of Coreopsis, a great variety of flowers might be found throughout the season. These include Fremont Phacelia, Cliffrose, Crested Onion, Desert Calico, Blue Dicks, Thistle Sage, several species of Gilia, Prince's Plume, Purple Mat, Fairy Trumpet, Scarlet Bugler, Silver Cholla, Beavertail Cactus, Brittlebush, Calif. Buckwheat, Paperbag Bush, Flat Top Buckwheat, Winter Fat, Cotton Thorn, Brittlebush, and Creosote Bush.

Area V. ANGELES FOREST HIGHWAY

This is a good area for mountain shrubs such as Manzanita, Chamise as well as for Our Lord's Candle, Live Forever and Mesa Phlox.

Area VI. LANCASTER

In the past we have seen large fields of Royal Desert Lupine and Desert Dandelion within the city limits of Lancaster. But these have now been covered with housing tracts. On 20th St. East and Ave L during some years, one can still find a variety of species including the Dune Primrose, Chinese Houses and Purple Mat.

Area VII. ANTELOPE VALLEY FREEWAY (Highway 14)

In the spring of the year it is not unusual to see fields of wildflowers on either side of the freeway. California Poppies sometimes cover the hills above Vincent (between Acton and Palmdale), a little further north, after the Angeles Forest Highway offramp are blankets of Tidy Tips.

Area VIII. GODDE PASS, ELIZABETH LAKE RD.
AND LEONA VALLEY

A tremendous variety of wildflowers can be found growing on the hills on the north side of Leona Valley and in the area of Godde Pass at the peak of the season. These include California Poppies, Coreopsis, Chia, Brown Eyed Primrose, Indian Paintbrush, Phacelia, Forget-Me-Not, Spencer Primrose, California Primrose, Mustard-like Primrose, Fremont Phacelia, Jewel Flower, and Scarlet Bugler just to mention a few of the more prominent ones.

Area IX. BOUQUET CANYON

Although the Canyon did not get its name from the wildflowers growing on its hillsides, it could well have. The most spectacular displays are of the Farewell To Spring coming sometime in May. Other flowers which add to the beauty of the Canyon in late spring are Indian Paintbrush, Buckwheat, Red Ribbons, Western Wallflower,Checker Bloom, Sticky Monkey Flower, Chinese Houses, Popcorn Flower, Pearly Everlasting, Amole, several species of Mariposa Lilies, Golden Ear Drops, Indian Pinks, Clematis, Chamise and absolute forests of Our Lord's Candle.

Area X. ELIZABETH LAKE (including Johnson Hill Road,
Munz Ranch Road, Lake Hughes and Pine Canyon Road.)

Approaching Elizabeth Lake through Johnson Hill Road (the south extension of 110th St. West) sometime in April, the visitor can be rewarded with whole hillsides covered with California Poppies and Coreopsis. Mixed in with these are Lupine, Globe Gilia, Jewel Flower, California Primrose, Chia and Spencer Primrose. Further west, on the north side of Elizabeth Lake, the same varieties of wildflowers can be seen in addition to white Tidy Tips, large Bush Lupine and Scarlet Bugler. Munz Ranch Road leading north reveals more Bush Lupine, Wooly Paintbrush and Baby Blue Eyes. Probably the most spectacular sight is of the fields of Owl's Clover (in wet years) and Califorina Poppies after crossing the California Aqueduct.

Area XI. SAN FRANCISQUITO RD. (Shay's Castle Rd.)

The dirt road running northwest off of Munz Ranch Road just north of the Aqueduct not only leads past Shay's Castle (an unusual enough sight by itself) but also through fields of Goldfields, Desert Dandelion, Owl's Clover, Thistle Sage, Filaree and California Poppies. In addition, there are many clumps of Wild Rhubarb, a scattering of Elegant Lupine and an occasional sighting of Red Maids. It takes a really close look to see the very tiny Hairy Lotus or some Keel Fruit blossoms The evening brings out fields of Evening Snow.

Area XII. CALIFORNIA STATE POPPY RESERVE

Every conscientious flower-watcher should visit the Jane S. Pinheiro Interpretive Center and walk the many trails of the "Poppy Park." Docents and park rangers will provide a great amount of information about the many flowers on the Reserve and the purpose of the Park. The most spectacular displays are of the Goldfields, the annual California Poppies and the Davy Gilia.

Area XIII. AVE D
(Highway 138 from 110th St. West to Gorman)

The large fields of California Poppies, Davy Gilia, Desert Dandelion, Lupine, Owl's Clover and Monolopia on both sides of Highway 138 are as spectacular as any around and should make any traveler want to stop awhile and smell the flowers.

Area XIV. 190TH ST. WEST TO 205TH ST. WEST
(southwest of the California Aqueduct)

At the corner of Lancaster Road and 190th St. West, continue going west. Follow the road across the Aqueduct to see an area containing the greatest variety of wildflowers of which I am aware. During a two-hour period in April of 1985, I was able to identify more that 40 different wildflowers. Prominent among them were Goldfields, Golden Gilia, Thistle Sage, Blue Sage, California Poppies, Parry Gilia, Desert Dandelion, Goldenbush, Blue Dicks, Phacelia, Pincushion, Scale Bud, Scarlet Bugler, Davy Gilia and California Primrose.

Area XV. GORMAN POST ROAD

A short distance west of Quail Lake on Highway 138, take the Gorman Post Road to the right to see one of the most beautiful wildflower vistas in the area. In the early season, the hills are carpeted with Coreopsis. Later come the California Poppy and large stands of Benthan Lupine, truly one of the most beautiful lupine anywhere. Many Bladder-Pod can be seen thoughout the area. Flower-watchers are unable to walk among these beautiful fields because they are behind fences and up the mountainside, but from the road they are truly spectacular.

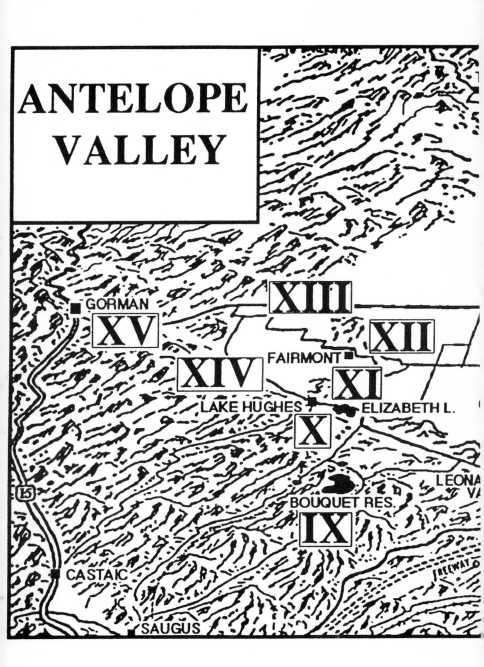

ANTELOPE VALLEY

GORMAN

XV

XIII

XII

FAIRMONT

XIV

XI

LAKE HUGHES

ELIZABETH L.

X

LEONA
VA

BOUQUET RES.

IX

⑤

CASTAIC

FREEWAY

SAUGUS